Praise for
WITHOUT WORDS

"In *Without Words*, Harvey Martin takes us on an elegant, soulful journey from who we were to who we are to who we can be. This barefoot walk into spirituality will change how you see the world and yourself."

—Tim Brown, two-time *New York Times* bestselling author

"My friend Harvey Martin has been working for years at the leading edge of human performance. In this book, he shares his new ways of thinking about and resolving some of the most fundamental questions that are critical to the actualization of human potential. For those seeking a deeper understanding of themselves and their relationship to the environments and experiences that help shape them, Martin's latest book will serve as an inspiring intellectual guide."

—Thomas P Seager, PhD, CEO of Morozko Forge

"*Without Words*, the latest book by Major League Baseball's human performance coach Harvey Martin, is an exploration of authenticity in an often disconnected and materialistic world. At its essence, this book is part memoir, part mirror, challenging the reader to dig deep and search the quiet recesses of the soul. What is our foundation? Is our life in balance with our intent? And how do we foster reconciliation? In *Without Words*, Martin inspires curiosity, stretching the reader. And to be comfortable in the silence of becoming. For it is in that quiet, without words or expectations, that the soul is filled and we find that which we seek."

—Amy Scanlin, MS, Wayfarer, Wordsmith, Bon Vivant

"In *Without Words*, Harvey Martin embraces the timeless yearning to know who and why we are. With skill and grace, he navigates depth and uncertainty, gifting us a real opportunity to peer calmly and deeply into the Self."

—Tommy La Stella, Chicago Cubs,
2016 World Series Champion,
2019 MLB All-Star

"*Without Words* takes you on a journey through the past to have a deeper understanding of humankind. This thought-provoking novel will have you asking yourself questions that put you more in touch with your soul."

—Mitch Haniger, Seattle Mariners, 2018 All-Star

"This book is an authentic deep dive into the meaning of life from a very open-minded perspective. *Without Words* supplies wisdom about the human organism on how we think, feel, and create. Harvey allows the reader to ponder why it is we are here and how that relates to god."

—Nick Bjugstad, Florida Panthers first round pick,
twelve-year NHL hockey player

Without Words :
Mastering the Art of Being

by Harvey Martin

© Copyright 2024 Harvey Martin

ISBN 979-8-88824-559-0

All rights reserved. No part of this publication may be reproduced, stored in a retrieval system, or transmitted in any form or by any means—electronic, mechanical, photocopy, recording, or any other—except for brief quotations in printed reviews, without the prior written permission of the author.

Published by

köehlerbooks™

3705 Shore Drive
Virginia Beach, VA 23455
800-435-4811
www.koehlerbooks.com

WITHOUT WORDS: MASTERING THE ART OF BEING

HARVEY MARTIN

VIRGINIA BEACH
CAPE CHARLES

DEDICATION

I dedicate this book to the curious. May we stumble as one as we seek to understand our nature.

TABLE OF CONTENTS

Introduction
Chapter 1..Dear Soul
Chapter 2...Abstract God
Chapter 3..Human Experience
Chapter 4..Hierarchical Power
Chapter 5..Philosophy
Chapter 6...Philosophy of Religion
Chapter 7..Natural World
Chapter 8..Sensory Experience
Chapter 9..Mind-Body Connection
Chapter 10...The Call

DEFINITIONS

Characters: Used to describe the physical mind and body.

Material: Used to describe physical reality in the third dimension.

Materialism: Tendency to consider material possessions and physical comfort more important than spiritual values.

Spiritual: Relating to or affecting the human spirit or soul as opposed to material or physical things.

Soul: Used to describe higher consciousness and higher dimensions.

INTRODUCTION

Who am I? It makes us wonder if it's possible to describe authenticity through words. We'd love to feel original, but the idea of being me is often the process of becoming you. We don't say what we think we are. We say what we think you think we are. Without knowing, the roles we play and the character we become are often the result of an environment that defines the "I" in our answer. To the contemplative mind, when we go beyond the surface of our material world, we are left without words.

This book focuses on the mechanics of being in the material world and discovering the soul. The material world will be defined throughout the text as our three-dimensional reality from birth to death. Within that context, we experience measurable time and acquire a personality. Through life, our personality is shaped by learning from experience, and we solidify a character. These mechanics within human psychology are to identify with what we know.

Whether we form our beliefs consciously or unconsciously, the laws of nature indicate we are meant to experience life with balance. This means our essence and personality should complement each other. By its very nature, modern life stifles the development of our essence, manipulating personality, and presents a disharmonious state of being in the third dimension. This forces a dysfunctional awareness that answers "Who am I?" with definitive words that confuse us and how we present ourselves to the world.

The "I" concept forms personalities by conforming to society's trends. Forever longing to share authenticity, the mirror of materialism leaves no room for error. Our environment tells us we must choose a character and become the personality attached to it. Still, that personality is often in direct conflict and causes friction with who we think we really are. We naturally become a species shackled with fear and lose the essence of our soul. Without an ability to explore, our environment curates our character in a process that eliminates wonder. Therefore, we bleed the opportunity for authentic ponder.

This book is designed to spark thinking and deepen a relationship with the soul. Personally, growing up Catholic in Midwestern America to a middle-class family, my narrative was spoken through public schools and sports. I performed my role, followed rules, and formed an identity. Getting a college degree, performing internships, and chasing the dollar was nothing unusual. Until one day, consciousness—as I knew it—broke down. No longer playing the avatar, I was faced with the depths of depression.

At the bottom of consciousness, a source holds the meetings for our characters' personalities. Awakening begins when the soul recognizes that the words we've been using to describe ourselves don't fit—we're none of them. Then, we meet with the soul in a space of nothing to discover essence. This is when we move beyond the surface and become comfortable without words. This new state of being reflects a presence in the character to know oneself, which directs the meaningful path of becoming whole.

A passage from *The Book of Zen* by Alan Watts sparked my enthusiasm to write this book. It launched a journey to share insights gathered from my experience, which feels connected to the souls of the twenty-first century. The passage reads, "No dependence upon words and letter; Direct pointing to the soul of man; Seeing into one's own nature."

I wrote this book years after saying goodbye to a character I once knew. Directly pointing to the soul, lingering in uncertainty, I feel I'm not alone. In a quest for wholeness, we stand in awe while our essence plays the characters of reality. It is my hope that the content in this book simply sparks an enthusiasm to experience life without justification and connect with the power of not knowing. With curiosity, may we stumble as one.

CHAPTER 1

DEAR SOUL

Who am I? With depths unconscionable to consider, we are oftentimes left without words as we shape our consciousness around the question. The mechanics of human nature are to classify objects to avoid uncertainty. We do this so we have something to believe in. Whether that's our religions or philosophies, we need something to provide structure. Therefore, the stories we share shape what we think we are. For instance, we are given a name, number, and lineage at birth—identifications that designate meaning to our mind and body—but to the soul, we are speechless.

In truth, we often fall short of connecting with the soul. We realize there is no lasting enlightenment within the material world, and our ambition goes unconscious. Our minds become fixed, contributing to why curiosity dies with age. We disconnect with our essence, and childlike tendencies fade. In time, our character reaches new levels. Whether through achievement, financial gain, or social status, we naturally fall into a relatively stable position of well-being, considered the hedonic treadmill.

Our high for material resources wears off, and we unconsciously embark on the next checkpoint, hoping to find the truth. This is an evolving lie to induce happiness through gain because we eventually retreat to baseline. Desire, however, paradoxically contributes to the exploration of the characters we play, and we discover the soul within the acts of our mind and body. We must, therefore, intend to harmoniously participate in the third dimension with our true essence while experiencing the vastness of human personality.

To build awareness, human nature, like a machine, works based on function. For instance, a person chooses a specific university to attend because that's where their family went. In this case, the individual avoids uncertainty while feeling obligated to fulfill the narrative of their family. Believing they are the character, the surrounding narrative creates a false purpose for the individual and keeps them on a treadmill. One must dismantle one's personality and ponder "Who am I?" to alleviate unnecessary suffering—which is an everlasting contemplation without words. In our lifetime, we cannot dismiss the exposure of playing the roles within society. However, we must comprehend the illusion that we experience. We might follow in our family's footsteps, but we are not the circumstances or personalities we acquire.

QUESTIONS

To dismantle one's personality, one must study oneself. Observing mechanics, we are met with questions to anticipate our arrival and build awareness. We are a curious species, contemplating who we are, and questions are the frontier to meaningful suffering. As our character rises in status, our understanding of success serves as the classroom for self-discovery. When we stop to question ourselves and reflect on who we are, we acquire the awareness needed to balance our personality with our soul's essence.

As we saw with our ancestors, curiosity led us out of Africa. The ability to question who we would become led our species to new territories, creating diversity in our thinking as the early explorers experienced unknowns. Our working minds created rituals and traditions and developed cultures with each adaptation to satisfy our characters. Constant progress and our need for survival forced us to work together through trade. Through the process, cultures impacted others, shaping and defining roles.

We created ease, and the space provided allowed us to spend more time in our minds. Time allowed conscious thinking to form language unlike any other species, and we had a unique ability to share knowledge. Scalability developed, and the fast-paced learning curve enabled generations to pass down the structure for survival, leading to longer lifespans and the most comfortable lifestyle any animal on Earth has witnessed. We trekked our way to a better life, and the result of the modern-day lifestyle became arguably the saddest, loneliest, and most confused generation of our time. If there are no more lands to explore and no more predators to conquer, the New Age war is within, making the next checkpoint in evolution a stalemate with consciousness. We now await a question to feed the soul.

To question "Who am I?" stops physical progression in the material world and grants us the necessary uncertainty for soulful adaptation. The question forces a crippling anxiety required in pursuit of discovering the "I" of ourselves. Accepting this subjective endeavor, we'll fight the world to learn we are the world, which builds an awareness that acknowledges existence without words. When we reach this point of recognition, we view our characters as a form of play. We will then perform roles effectively, realizing the path to self-discovery is balancing our character's performance with recognition of the soul.

IDENTITY

The soul is beyond the characters we play. We play the role of Christianity, Hinduism, or Buddhism. We speak the language of Aristotle and Socrates. We set out to build our Roman Empires while yearning for simple living. We dance under the stars and talk to the trees. Searching for adventure, we chain ourselves to comfort. We become marveled by magic but need facts.

Trapped with perspective, we can't honestly know reality. Our deficiencies force madness, and we create a structure to massage fear. The repetitive nature advertises our existence from the surface because, to be authentic, we enter the depths of our souls, which are too vulnerable to reveal to the tribe. We are terrified that the world will find our shortcomings, so we identify with the characters we play as truth. This is a perspective of false identification we'll use to operate within the confines of society. If we live on the surface, we'll fight wars to defend our image.

On a shared quest to alleviate pain, what happens when we take off the mask of our personality and consider the soul? By removing oneself from the surface, the soul has an original experience in a world of illusion. We have no character to play and no act to perform. By seeking one's nature, we're freed from the chains of duality. We experience energy beyond the character and realize we're nothing. This defines our awareness's abstract belief; only the soul can accept this fate.

A conscious mind cannot allow things to be nothing. Therefore, the function of our mind attaches stories and systems that create how we want nothing to be. However, the soul finds life in infinite possibilities, leaving our learning process to the understanding that the act of being human is to play in society with the contracts our structure provides. Society will naturally shape and refine our character to play within the rules.

Our identity spiritually grows through the suffering of material structure, directly pointing us to our essence. From birth to death, our avatar treks through measurable checkpoints. It will adapt in the form of questions, and we'll answer as we are. As we wake up, the soul exposes our identity with no past nor future while we live in the exact moment of consciousness. When these awakenings occur periodically throughout life, we shed who we think we are. Arising in new states of being, change in perspective is our pursuit of becoming whole.

SUFFERING

The human experience is a struggle that catalyzes discovery; therefore, we suffer. Suffering is needed to make sense of the duality surrounding our being. Human nature needs this balance to find itself. Oscar Wilde said, "When the bankers get together for dinner, they discuss art. When artists get together for dinner, they discuss money." Using this analogy, to grow fully, we must play the role of both the banker and the artist.

Consequently, we must participate in life by exploring duality. For this reason, connecting with a higher being is reasonable to guide our paths. For years, spiritual teachers like priests, gurus, and shamans have directed our paths to connect with something bigger than ourselves. To alleviate suffering, the goal has been to give our species faith.

Depending on our awareness, we experience suffering at opposite ends of the spectrum. With material suffering, we feel like we are never enough as we run on the treadmill. This level of suffering keeps us feeling inadequate and meaningless. With spiritual suffering, we struggle through pain, but it gives us meaning. We recognize that we are never enough, and paradoxically, we're fueled with purpose. On that account, we can detach from the characters we play and live with intention.

When we connect with the soul, we move beyond the time of birth-to-death experience. Within material reality, we become a spiritual being having a human experience. The who or what we are cannot only be the mind and body character because we exist connected to an essence. Therefore, we must exist beyond our physical comprehension of what we perceive as reality.

Our awareness plays characters guiding our souls through a human experience. For example, when we are in the state of being a student, we are learning. When we are in the state of being a parent, we are nurturing. These are not achievements but rather states of being. In our present moment, we are playing the role and immersed in character.

Consider a hotel receptionist. The receptionist is performing the character of someone who greets others. They update the hotel records and ensure each guest is checked in or out. They keep track of these records and maintain the structure of guest services. The quality in which someone plays the character is based on their appearance, body language, and the tone of their voice. If the hotel receptionist can respond quickly and professionally and maintain politeness, they are perceived as a quality character. The hotel receives higher reviews and financial growth, and it is in management's best interest to hire the utmost character.

The state of being, however, is matched with becoming and our state of nothingness. The hotel receptionist cannot be the receptionist. He or she performing the character is not the role. To be whole, the receptionist must exist in a state of nothingness beyond the illusion. The hotel guests, therefore, experience solely the performance the receptionist can deliver. Yet, the receptionist's is balanced with nothing because there is no receptionist. It is a role a person plays, an illusion.

The soul inside the character is consumed with a conundrum of nothingness. There is no requirement or standard for a receptionist to remain a receptionist. Nothing within material reality stops the exploration of their nothingness. However, in a society clinging to structure, we can only perform roles at the surface of what we consider objective. This is how we establish rules to uphold behaviors that allow us to play together.

However, beyond the roles we play, we are nothing. We are limitless, expressing authenticity through our consciousness. Oscar Wilder's quote rings true because the banker must not only discuss art to experience the edges of being and becoming. They need to become it. Similarly, for the artists to make money, they cannot only discuss it. They need to become it.

Material suffering arises when we believe we are solely the character. The banker who believes themselves to be the banker never explores the state of nothingness. They won't experience life beyond their character, which inevitably limits their potential as a banker. Similarly, you see this issue with the starving artists. Artists are often comfortable playing the character of nothingness. They explore the world in terms of subjectivity. With no structure and constant spontaneity, they create beautiful works of art but cannot make money until learning the banker's character. We do this because we materially identify ourselves to be one thing.

Our material perspective is filled with insecurities and weakness, enslaving us to our impurities. On the other side of tangible, spiritual suffering is wholeness. We realize that we are here to experience personality through our societal roles. With constant evolution, we exercise our skills within the characters we play. We know that we are not just the banker or the artist; we are both.

CHAPTER 2

ABSTRACT GOD

Fear overwhelms the character because we struggle to live without justification, which forces us toward faith. Finding trust in an unexplainable source somehow makes us feel justified. God, our solution, is utterly independent and the source of actual reality. Often considered the presence of life, faith is a feeling. For instance, Yahweh, a Hebrew name for God, is regarded by the Jewish people as a name too sacred to be spoken.

In the material world, the human experience is three-dimensional. The X, Y, and Z axes are the defining materials of length, width, and depth of all objects in the universe. These are essential measurables that feed our structure and where we connect with our mind and body. We can't comprehend energy associated with further dimensions; therefore, we struggle to articulate who and what God is.

Only the power of the soul can go beyond material and deal with its infinity. For example, we know the Milky Way exists in space—but not space. Comparable to a mathematical constant, we know equations—but not mathematics. Our abstract sciences are applied to disciplines such as physics and engineering to provide structure in the third dimension. Parallel to the multiple ideas about God, we structure the experience. However, the creator remains unsolvable.

Accordingly, a constant process of surrendering to nothingness and letting go of our need to justify God must occur. In our search for answers, creation contains mystery in questions, and the only truth we've uncovered as a species is that we know nothing. Together, by knowing nothing, we experience fear.

INTERPRETATION

We lean on the theory that we are human beings experiencing reality, whereas the source gives reality the experience of us. We cannot be this mind and body in the presence of God. Therefore, only our interpretation of the material justifies reality in the third dimension. Our timelines are measurable in matter, and we recognize the structure of people, places, and objects. The issue with our interpretation of the material world is that we base everything on memory. Therefore, we don't see reality; we see our reality. This perspective chains us to material suffering because our senses stimulate feedback loops to what we believe is true. For example, our eyes and ears take in electrical signals, which our brains interpret based on expectations.

Consider the variety of trauma among individuals. A soldier returning from war could be triggered by the sound of a lawn mower, replaying the sounds of explosions or gunshots in their past. At the same time, another person only finds the lawn mower annoying and closes the window. In this analogy, we can reference our disconnect from reality, but it is also an analogy to how we perceive God. We can't define our interpretation of reality to anyone, which makes the intention of worshipping a God meaningful. We feel understood when we connect with the source, but it makes God abstract.

Based on interpretation, we unconsciously fall into habits that structure our perspective. As we survey the world with our own interpretation, how likely is it that we worship the same God? For instance, in the Christian Bible, God is a "He" and represents all humans. The Taoism God is considered oneness, a belief that humans and animals should live in balance with the universe.

STRUCTURED GOD

Without answers, our soul seeks the experience of being human. Not to be intertwined with the character that needs structure, spiritual revelation happens the further we investigate material and make our lives a form of play. The soul can then be relinquished from human need, allowing the three-dimensional experience to be met with limited attachment to the character.

In our search for meaning, the longer we grip material, the more significant the gap between us and God. Therefore, we must be open to everything and attached to nothing. To do this, we turn to the child, where existence is enough. The child's character is filled with wonder. They remain in a constant state of creating and learning the self. As they explore, children remain naturally curious and connected to God. Revelation of the soul is the journey of gathering scars in the material world with our childlike curiosity. As we pursue potential through life's tests, we walk to God.

Freedom is the leap of faith we take upon our walk. When we get to this point, we tap into the revelation. Finding inspiration, we become stimulated to create, as a child does. A state of mind that only happens in the presence of God. A presence that eliminates our character's fear and sets us free from the duality of the material world. When we exercise faith in the material, we experience the form of play our soul needs to evolve.

When faced with temptation, focusing on problems of the material world disconnects us from God. Fighting for possessions, the war for resources can quickly consume our character. Studying history, as we conquered a globe, fighting for material possessions, our characters frequently lied, thinking we could play God. Trusting man-made governments and hierarchical systems as fact. We used such powers to create and enforce rules in the third dimension. Often fixed through the law, we blindly handed faith to narratives acting as God.

The material world provides government policies to structure and develop a defense. It needs to govern foreign affairs, public services, and the economy in which we live. That being so, we see power dynamics as tangible. As a result, the mechanics of our mind unconsciously structure God when we go to the churches and jobs our government provides. Placing faith in materialism that fits the classification of our interpretation of God may soothe our mind, but it disrupts the essence of our soul. Therefore, the character must play in the material world while surrendering to infinity. This builds an awareness of moving beyond structure in the third dimension to discover the soul.

GOD AND GOVERNMENT

Our obsession with structure tranquilizes unknowns. It is the reason investors want a solid business plan or the explanation that justifies the value of an athlete. If we can measure something, we can manage it. The ability to build structure around hierarchy, religion, and philosophy serves as the measurable qualities to ensure order among humanity. With established laws and curricula, we give grounds to right versus wrong. This forces the decisions of both individuals and groups to be held accountable for the greater good. If we don't enforce structure, we have no foundation for survival. Our issue arises when we do the same thing with God. If our character forms a structure around an infinite source, we misinterpret nothingness and dismiss the faith needed for our soul's evolution.

The abstract feeling of faith is too much for our character, so we develop a hierarchy in our systems built from the mechanics of our minds. For example, "In God We Trust" is printed on all United States of America currency, making an alliance visible to the citizens and people printing the money. If God establishes the leaders of governments, we can follow humans under the impression that they are led by God. This is a viable solution to quiet our fears and trust a structured system. We do this because it aligns with the functions of the human mind.

Throughout history, rulers have advertised themselves as appointed prophets, and the ordinary citizen obliged. Genghis Khan said, "I am the punishment of God. If you had not committed great sins, God would not have sent a punishment like me upon you." Genghis Khan and the Mongols are associated with terrible tales of conquest and bloodshed. Near the turn of the thirteenth century, the famous clan leader, Khan, created the largest empire ever to exist, simultaneously causing mass destruction to lands and people among them. If what he was saying is true, the question becomes, was he led by God?

In the Christian Bible, God revealed principles in scripture to help guide Christians on matters pertaining to rule. With the understanding that God established government, the Lord's sovereign reign over the world included the establishment of human authorities. From the Bible verse Romans 13:1 (NAB): "Let every person be subordinate to the higher authorities, for there is no authority except from God, and those that exist have been established by God." Romans 13: 2 (NAB): "Therefore, whoever resists authority opposes what God has appointed, and those who oppose it will bring judgment upon themselves."

The government was instituted by God to command good, punish evil, and maintain peace. Throughout the Old Testament, the appointed Prophets and Apostles from God were empowered and directed to obey God. If they remained obedient, God would use them to help govern the people.

The story of Moses, within the Torah, is the second of five books of the Hebrew Bible. He was a significant prophet of the Jewish God Yahweh. He led the Israelites out of slavery and established the first laws for the Israelite society. At the time, the Israelites were enslaved in Egypt by the Pharaoh after initially going to escape famine. Moses went to the Pharaoh and ordered he let the Israelites go, as Yahweh commanded. The Pharaoh did not accept, and Yahweh demonstrated his power by sending ten plagues into Egypt. Eventually, the Pharaoh's son was killed during one of the plagues, and he let the Israelites go.

Once the people left for the Promised Land, the Pharaoh changed his mind and went after them. Bringing an army of chariots, they quickly caught the Israelites traveling by foot. The Israelites regretted leaving Egypt and were overwhelmed with fear. As they pushed forward and reached the Red Sea, they lost hope. At that moment, Yahweh directed Moses to stretch out his hand over the waters to part the sea, allowing the Israelites to walk across.

Once across, Moses was directed to release the waters and drown the Egyptians who were chasing behind. Moses's acts expressed Yahweh's power, and the Israelites won their freedom. In an event known as the Exodus, the Israelites ensured their exit from Egypt and made their way to the wilderness. Following the escape, Yahweh gave Moses the task of leading the Israelites to the "Promised Land."

Along the way, Moses received the Ten Commandments from Yahweh, establishing the basis for Jewish law. If we draw a connection to these stories, we see that a ruler appointed by God established the law.

WORSHIP

Worship is the expression of reverence and adoration for a deity. It is a reaction to an action. Once God is revealed and creates the action of revelation, the response from an individual or group occurs with worship. It is a position of humility and surrender in which we allow the source to work through us. The Israelites followed Moses because they saw the powers God gave him. The laws brought to them through the commandments were an act of God, not necessarily Moses.

Even today, we find ourselves wanting to worship God and not people. Without words, we worship when we believe we've seen what we're searching for. These are the moments when we move beyond the material world. We detach from the character and connect with the soul.

Worship has a variety of styles. Some find worship through music. Religious practice believes worship is within traditional church ceremonies, such as baptism or communion, and many people find worship personal and individual. The Mayans built pyramids to worship their gods. The Kiva, used by our Ancestral Puebloans, is a small hole in the floor that allows spirits to enter. During travel in the wilderness, the people of Israel were commanded to build tabernacles so God could "dwell among them" (Exodus 29:46).

Praise differs in that it applauds what God or the gods have done. When we praise our higher powers, our character boldly declares. In soulful worship, it humbly bows. Praise is instead a subset of prayer and more encouragement upon what has been accomplished. We can praise anyone or anything for the good things they've done because it's measurable.

Worship is soulful, a moment when we devote our energy to dimensions beyond. We bow down in recognition that there's something more significant than the character. Without words, worship becomes sacred and meaningful. However, in congruence with society's melting pot, we are diverse in our ways of worship. Much of how we decide to worship comes through tradition and the specific religion we practice.

With intentions to maintain a relationship with the holy, we attend different places to worship. Variety is explored—where Jewish worship is in a synagogue, Christian worship is in a church. Religions such as Hinduism, Buddhism, Shintoism, and many ancient faiths worship in temples. Islam prayer takes place in mosques or a Muslim house of worship. These all serve as sacred places representing spiritual connection. Just as we structure law through government, we structure connection through worship and prayer.

PRAYER & MEDITATION

Guidance in the religious community considers prayer an essential part of life. The line of communication is directly with God. From healing the sick to asking for forgiveness, these are acts in which one connects with the divine. Whether requesting help or expressing thanks, prayer can be individual and communal. Using words or songs, prayer can even be in complete silence. Using language or seeking guidance, we sometimes take prayer as hymns or formal creedal statements.

History tells us the act of prayer dates back 5,000 years and is traditionally practiced during the morning or evening and over meals for grace. Bowing our heads and folding our hands is the image of the Christian religion. Hindus chant mantras, and Native Americans dance. Muslims are required to pray five times a day while facing the Kaaba in Mecca. Rabbinical Judaism made it customary for Jews to pray three times a day while emphasizing special days such as the Shabbat and Jewish holidays.

Meditation differs slightly because it is considered a moment to connect with yourself. By directing energy inward, the intention is comparable to prayer in that the individual seeks spiritual clarity. However, meditation does not use a God or deity as the focal point and is often considered a moment to ponder. Eastern religions such as Buddhism and Shintoism are accompanied by meditation.

Though differing in styles, most, if not all, humans have some form of meditation. The practice is to be focused on one thing, typically the breath or a thought. The individual starts by paying attention to each breath or repeating a mantra repetitively in their mind, with many forms to guide pondering, such as silent walking, imagery, or mindfulness. Even going into nature is a form of meditation. Furthermore, tuning into your surroundings through sound, visuals, and touch are all forms of practice.

Meditation is likely to have begun with humanity itself. Some historians believe it started around 3000 BCE; however, the earliest records of meditation are attributed to the Hindu Vedas around 1500 BCE (Sharma 2015). Other documents, such as the Torah, contain descriptions in Genesis when the patriarch Isaac goes to "Lasuach" in a field. A kind of Jewish meditation most likely practiced around 1000 BCE (Kaplan 1985).

Believed to have originated in India, meditation spread worldwide and integrated into religions and spiritual practices. Evolving around 600 and 400 BCE within Taoist China and Buddhist India (Bronkhorst 2014), Buddha became famously recognized for the art of meditation. He produced a key ingredient to the movement when he coined "Monkey Mind."

Buddha believed the mind was held by drunken monkeys jumping around, clinging from tree to tree while endlessly talking nonsense chatter. The metaphor curated his teaching, meditation, in which he taught his students to relax the mind and tame the monkey. In silence, focused on breathing, Buddha explained the monkey's mind would quiet and become calm. Once the students became calm, they would see the world clearly and move toward enlightenment.

ENLIGHTENMENT TRAP

Our characters are filled with cluttered minds, and we become information seekers because of them. Trapped in pursuit of perfection, we seek to know what God knows and be enlightened and free from paradoxical chains as we consume what we interpret as proper knowledge. To the character, we would be enlightened and free from the bond of material suffering if we consume the proper knowledge.

For many reasons, we've found strength in religion. With different styles, we're similar in our practices because we don't know what happens in the afterlife. Therefore, within material suffering, we'll go to great lengths to prove the mystical powers of the universe—a perspective that produces more suffering in our inability to accept nothingness.

A story from the Christian Bible shares these insights with the narrative of Adam and Eve. As told, the serpent persuaded Eve to eat from the *tree of knowledge*, convincing Eve she would know what God knows. This was an enlightenment trap, as Eve took the temptation. After eating the apple, Adam followed in her footsteps, and the two went from a spirit to a physical body. Now able to see each other's nakedness, they created a state of judgment while being insecure of themselves. Forming duality, sin was placed among the people of God for their lack of obedience. It is a story in which God teaches the character to trust in the unknown without forcing the need to justify.

Another enlightenment trap occurred around 567 BCE. In a small kingdom below the Himalayan foothills, Buddha was born. The Brahmins prophesied that he would become a universal monarch or a great sage. However, his father feared he would become ascetic, so he kept him in the confines of the family palace. Siddhartha Gautama, the "Buddha," grew up in luxury, shielded from the outside world. One day, guided to believe in perfection and enamored with pleasures, his own shadow drew him beyond the castle walls.

In the streets, he encountered three eye-opening perspectives: a sick man, an old man, and a corpse being carried to the burning grounds. Buddha, who knew nothing but ease, was unprepared for the experience. With a new perspective, Buddha could not rest. He left the palace in search of answers to suffering. Confused, he rode off and realized that conditioned experiences could not provide lasting happiness or protect us from suffering. His search led him to deep silence, where he discovered the nature of our material mind. Eventually, he created the noble truths and taught his students that suffering was inevitable. This story highlights the pain of our human experience needed to recognize our soul.

CHAPTER 3

HUMAN EXPERIENCE

Time rewards the experience of trying on the characters of the mind and body. From the moment we are born, these experiences shape our awareness. Made tangible through the development of our character, reality teaches us the perfect storm of chaos and control. In pursuit of nothingness, we are handed our path of suffering. To be human is to experience duality and learn how to surrender. Letting go of attachment to the material is our soul's way of moving beyond the surface of our character so that we can spiritually suffer.

The material world guides the human experience with structure as an avenue to direct the path of discovery. There is a framework to the experience that includes feelings and behaviors we need to discover within our characters. The framework of what we can see and touch is how we form our roles. It is also how we attach meaning to the structure of society. For this reason, it is important not to dismiss the material experience because we must use the structured path to learn who we are.

Considering the framework, imagine looking into a mirror. Imagine how you appear and notice how you feel inside. You begin to see what you seem to be. When we think about human nature, the imagination of self through the mirror is the same. As a species, we look into the mirror to check our identity. We investigate the nature of feelings to understand how we get them. When we understand the patterns of behavior, we can reach the capacity of our characters' expression.

As a group, we are interconnected and developed cultures, religions, and races to help define who we are. Intentionally moving as the alchemist within time, our experience requires we share the gifts of adaptation. This creates a paradox because our lives are about questions and not answers—an ongoing system that corrupts our ability to sustain a firm definition of who we are. Since we find no truth in the material, we only pick up knowledge that guides adaptation toward nothingness.

AGREE TO DISAGREE

With the seeds of peculiarity, our questioning drives debate, which has led to much of the world's conflict and our unease with the state of nothing. We've tried curiosity approaches, tracing questioning philosophy back to the roots of ancient Greece, an intellectual time when early philosophers loved the concept of questions. They wanted to ask the big questions and often did not concern themselves with the need for an answer.

Assuming that the process of debate is to advance the species further into the unknown, with established ground rules, questions such as 'Who is God?' would have to result in no answer. We would agree structurally to live without words because the answers to such questions are too abstract—and don't fit within society's structure. Thinking can't collectively grasp the illusion of life; therefore, we've failed in debate.

Instead, we debate cultural identities and laws against others as truth. If we can touch and see structure, we accept it since anxiety gets silenced with answers. We crave the comfort of a solidified image so immensely that we'll fight each other to defend these truths, reiterating the paradox, because we can't share each other's interpretations. So, we argue like chattering monkeys.

We meet resistance when trying to accept our state of nothing. Armoring ourselves with beliefs, values, and principles to justify our lives. Without control of truth, anxiety alters the course of decisions and dismantles the character of society's progress. The lesson is for the character to be able to acknowledge the rules of society but follow them without attachment. To sit in a space of nothingness and direct intention from the soul.

Debating without answers requires an awareness that balances dualism, and we cannot climb without balance. Therefore, to build strength, we dive into the history of our characters. We can see ourselves in the mirror as we better understand time. Beginning with evolution and language development, we can draw confidence from learning about our past. In a world of change, our interconnected nature requires inclusion and the ability to agree to disagree.

HUMAN EVOLUTION

The basis of our story is the process in which human beings evolved on Earth from now-extinct primates. With Africa as our first home, we adapted to a diverse group of monkeys, lemurs, and apes. On average, our DNA is 96 percent identical to our most distant primate relatives and nearly 99 percent to our closest relatives, the chimpanzees and bonobos (American Museum of Natural History, n.d.). Our extinct Homo habilis and Homo erectus species lived millions of years ago with skill sets in stone tools, skills that both chimpanzees and bonobos are competent in today.

Our original species are considered the first of our relatives to have humanlike body proportions, migrate out of Africa, and potentially cook food. Archaic Homo sapiens showed up around 300,000 years ago, and within 100,000 years, the modern Homo sapiens appeared. Homo sapiens, a Latin term for "wise man," is considered the species our modern character belongs to.

It was Carolus Linnaeus who first described our species in 1758 as Homo sapiens. However, Charles Darwin is primarily credited with the discovery of human evolution. His work stands at the foundation of modern evolutionary studies. An English naturalist, he developed a scientific theory of evolution called natural selection, a concept used to describe populations adapting to their environments over time. The basic idea is that populations and species of organisms change due to biological evolution.

The Homo sapiens were the only one of its kind to survive the dramatic climate change that took place thousands of years ago. These sapiens could adapt and sustain biological changes within the environment to keep them alive. According to Darwin, adaptations such as these are termed "survival of the fittest." The term suggests that organisms best adjusted to their environment are the most successful in surviving.

An essential survival mechanism of sapiens resides in their bigger brains and conscious behavior. The character's consciousness established species specialized in toolmaking and symbolic thinking, skills that helped adapt to new conditions and explore environments. Sapiens could roam Earth while taking every opportunity to adjust. With abundant space and resources, bigger brains acquire deep thinking and problem-solving skills to survive.

With a two-million-year incubation, consciousness built a character who thought, moved, and connected differently with the lands. Intelligence and the ability to walk upright on two legs created movement patterns that could be adjusted to handle variety in nature. The unique patterns allowed sapiens to climb trees, use their hands, and express flexibility, making them capable of changing habitats. These qualities and natural abilities needed to exist to continue evolution. Survival was no longer about being the biggest. It was about being the smartest.

Above all, the superpower came from the mind. To modern-day humans, sapiens have a large and complex brain. With expressed and advanced thinking and communicating symbols such as images, numbers, and letters, those far outweighed any other competitors' traits. The mind developed our ability to think, learn, and communicate to control the environment. Even today, these driving factors make the human experience different from other species.

In the beginning, this was the sapiens' edge. Consciousness grew, and we established awareness. We became aware enough to create religions, philosophies, and politics. Working together, building defense, and ruling lands, the art of communicating evolved.

STORYTELLING

With the growing development of our character, about 70,000 years ago, an epic journey began. Homo sapiens walked out of Africa and into the Middle East as a force to be reckoned with. Curious, each generation would go further in exploration and adaptation. Taking thousands of years and countless generations to cover Earth, our early ancestors experienced drastic change and were equipped for it. Great distances would be covered, taking the sapiens as far as what would become known as Australia and the Americas. Learning new terrain and weather patterns and being exposed to the world, we branched off from the animal kingdom as the first species to develop complex thinking and movement to handle all environments.

This era is primarily considered the cognitive revolution, highlighting our ability to think and communicate. For nearly

40,000 years, sapiens began speaking in a way the world had not seen. Relatively unknown to how it started, the idea is that a gene mutation changed how the brain was wired. Communication in the general sense was not the difference because apes, monkeys, dolphins, and even parrots communicate with each other. It was the complexity that separated the sapiens.

The sapiens created flexibility in their language. They could not only alarm the tribe that predators were nearby but also describe the exact location and how to attack and trap them. As you can imagine, this newly formed brain—a sort of high-tech animal—rose to the top of the food chain, turning the sapiens into fierce competition as they could work together with an efficiency that no other species could match. Life became more manageable, and the lack of competition awarded time. Time developed a space in which the sapiens used to gossip. For thousands of years, the concept of gossip meant continuation. Can you tell me which characters I can and cannot trust?

Today, much of the emotion surrounding gossip is negative. For sapiens, it was essential. Gossip was a form of language to convey information about others and a way to build trust. As the sapiens established cooperation, they needed gossip to grow their advantage. Trust became the foundation for survival. Gossip was used to help each other avoid working or cooperating with the wrong person or tribe. Even today, we use these tactics to make decisions by asking for recommendations and résumés. We start the process of gossip so we further the certainty of progress. We only trust those with whom we believe we share the same values. We do this to avoid strangers who may be undependable or do harm to us. Many of these actions are how we form our truths.

With flexibility, space, and gossip, one final piece of communication sparked the imagination of generations to come. The sapiens' complexity in speech formed fiction. The art of storytelling was born, and those who owned the power to control the campfire's tone controlled the group's cooperation. Through storytelling, the sapiens birthed the foundational beliefs into the impressionable minds near them. They found common ground through fiction and created meaning with social constructs and imagined realities. Sapiens were the first animals to discuss topics that didn't have a physical presence.

Examples of today are human rights, corporations, and God. This may not seem necessary for early existence, but where it paid off for sapiens is the meeting of common ground. If groups of people could cooperate under shared assumptions and goals, they would improve their chances of survival. We use these same qualities to defend our religions and philosophies.

Even now, we must challenge our beliefs and the stories we hear. We must consider if stories are true or if we have chosen to believe them to share communion. Without dismissing the stories, our moral compass is curated from the traditions that give us meaning. We must question what has been passed down through society's structure.

POPULATION INCREASE

Community growth was essential to the sapiens because it increased the likelihood of survival. The early explorers found safety in numbers, and as the numbers grew, it became necessary to establish an order that required obedience. Hierarchy and protection allowed for an increase in numbers, which meant more safety. The global population grew gradually until the Common Era and was never a concern.

For about sixteen centuries, however, the population increased under our awareness before drastically speeding up in the nineteenth century. From a slow pace to a massive acceleration, we saw a steep rise in the twentieth century. The population explosion resulted from our advancement in scientific, technological, agricultural, and industrial revolutions. Numbers were now becoming a problem for the modern species.

Within that formation, we can point somewhere between 10,000 to 15,000 years ago when the agriculture phase emerged. We discovered ways to produce more food and generated the energy available to support more significant numbers of people in the prehistoric transition from hunting and gathering to settled agriculture. As hunting and gathering died off and humans could settle into a territory permanently, the nomadic lifestyle turned into homesteads and farming, triggering a massive change in society regarding the characters we played.

Complex language allowed imagination to form in our minds, whereas settlement and reliable food sources established the birth of civilizations. In time, exploration slowed, and we started seeing a reproduction boom. From the beginning, humans never seemed concerned about Earth's capacity. At least not until 1804, when the population reached one billion people. At the beginning of the nineteenth century, everything seemed to accelerate when the next billion came in only 123 years. From then, a billion people have been added over much shorter periods. Soon, one billion people were added in only twelve years. Eventually, our population went from five to six billion, and only another twelve years needed to shift from six to seven billion. Scientists projected similar expectations to reach eight billion.

In the twentieth century, trade, communication, technological, and transportation advancements hastened the progress of humankind. The resulting progress was called globalization, a phrase used by economists to describe the world's first significant period of trade and finance. Historians consider it to have begun at the end of the fifteenth century, but many of today's scholars and theorists concentrate on a more recent past. If we consider modern history beginning 70,000 years ago, when the sapiens started the journey to the Middle East, this could be the beginning of the globalized connection.

As groups formed, trades needed to take place. Small civilizations developed commercial routes and experienced cultural exchanges to survive. As the influence of stories began to impact different tribes, you can imagine the confusion this had on the soul of a character. The sapiens learned diversity within their characters for the first time and performed the act of conformity to survive. As the population rises today, we are similarly tempted not to say what we think we are but instead what we believe the environment thinks we are. Conforming within small tribes, however, seems minimal compared to the modern character interconnected with the globe.

WAR AND CONFLICT

History is primarily painted through war. Stemming from inevitable suffering and our need to continue, we often experience conflict with each other. When we first roamed the earth, life was harsh. It was a priority to obtain food and shelter to sustain ourselves. Learning to work efficiently and in groups, an effective tactic was to trade resources with others. Interconnectedness was needed, and paradoxically, conflicts arose over resources. It wasn't the animals that created competition; it was the human-on-human crime that generated conflict. Land, food, and shelter all became valuable assets.

In 2015, *Time* wrote an article titled "Is World Peace Possible?" World peace means having an effective consensus regarding shared sacrifices and voluntary cooperation. Considering shared sacrifices, we would need to have the same fight to achieve peace. For example, many scientists believe the fight is the upcoming war we have with global warming. Expectations are of a large-scale impact occurring around 2030, with its peak by 2050, as we continue to burn coal, oil, and natural gas. Ultimately, the effect would challenge the existence of humans.

As we expanded our industrial activities and cleared land for agriculture, the world noticed an increase in greenhouse gas concentrations, raising atmospheric carbon dioxide levels. In 2022, the United Nations of Human Rights declared climate change the most significant threat the world has ever known.

Our species has faced threats before, experiencing war, scarcity, and pandemics. Plagues such as the bubonic plague or Black Death during the fourteenth century killed more than one-third of Europe—twenty-five million people. Another example is the New World smallpox from the 1520s to early 1600s when the first European settlers arrived on American shores. The Spanish ships brought a virus into present-day Mexico that killed nearly 90 percent of indigenous people. The yellow fever epidemic of 1793 remains one of the deadliest public health crises in American history, causing terror and economic disruption while taking 10 percent of the Philadelphia population in a matter of months.

In 2020, the globe was exposed to COVID-19, a global crisis. The pandemic kept the world indoors and forced a worldwide shutdown as health-care systems were overwhelmed. Social distancing and masks covered the faces of the world's population.

UP AHEAD

We are in a constant state of worry about the future. Accordingly, our search for answers is the desire to silence the feelings we experience from anxiety. A looming fear of where we got our next meal, how to prepare for the weather, or whether we would be attacked was inevitable for our ancestors. The constant need to be on the lookout undoubtedly placed a heavy dose of anxiety on the early mind. The innate survival mechanisms built fight-or-flight systems, saving us from predators while our complex brains taught us to work together.

Today, mental health movements scour the globe for tactics and lifestyle hacks to alleviate our characters' anxiety. In search of the soul, our conscious minds chose instead to produce food faster and find shelter. In pursuit of safety, we became comfortable, which appeased our character. We may not fear running from the lion anymore, but the mechanism still exists in our hardwiring. We have the same networks running through our present-day character as our ancestors. We remain programmed to run when things feel scary, and emotions are triggered by uncertainty.

The modern mind stops fear through escape. Rather than leaning into our state of nothing, we cope through comfort. We explore the world from the surface as we run to vacation and have our food delivered to the doorstep of our homes. We've developed technology that acquires resources in excess, and, as a result, our characters have become obese and burned out. We move less and think more, opposite our ancestral brothers and sisters. Even worse, we experience an overwhelming inundation of global issues. This New Age problem keeps our species in a steady panic—whether it's the confusing information about COVID-19, the war between Russia and Ukraine, or the conflict between Israel and Palestinians. If you are a character of the world, you are impacted by the narrative.

CHAPTER 4

HIERARCHICAL POWER

Anywhere we look in the modern world, society is ruled by power. What family you were born into or how well you're connected influences your position. Our character's hierarchy is known as Abraham Maslow's hierarchy of needs. The most essential elements for survival are physical: eating, drinking, sleeping, and safety. After these needs are met, humans require a sense of belonging and love. Following these necessities, we require confidence and esteem, which lead to self-actualization.

Our hierarchy makes us who we are and grants us creativity, values, and acceptance. Recognizing the structure of self maintains obedience to health, and when we honor the vitality of our organism's structure, we formulate a space for exploring our soul. This means the character has a hierarchy of needs to abide by to experience the material world. By mastering one's needs, we have power over the self, which floods our experience with abundance.

As an interconnected globe, our structure within groups focuses on the authority between people, such as governments, nations, states, and organizations. The dynamics can even work themselves into belief systems, such as religion. In America, for example, the top-down government begins with the president of the United States. The ranking system goes to the President, Vice President, House Speaker, Senate President, and Secretary of State. A religious example could be the hierarchy of the Roman Catholic Church. From highest to lowest: Pope, cardinals, archbishops, bishops, priests, and deacons. A family tree starts with our first ancestors, who were at the top, and eventually, their children. Then the children had children, and so on, until our family produced us, making each of us the child of two distinct genetic parents. As each person has a child, they continue the process. Mastering these processes is the intention behind hierarchy and our path to actualization.

We've developed these hierarchies to survive and maintain order among each other. Power gets formed from the top down, involving the decision-makers in choosing the group's direction. This way, a hierarchy organizes and guides progress among nations. Historically, this has created confusion in the mechanics of our minds because, materially, how likely is it that we know what is best for each other? We have routinely failed in our sense of belonging and love for one another. With eras of segregation, war, and conflict, our actualization of power has led to propaganda and the fall of empires. In our disconnect from communicating without words and our need for survival, the material suffering of reality clogs the awareness of individuals, stunting the abundance of humanity.

How we landed the importance of hierarchy is debatable and somewhat subjective. However, a wealth of evidence indicates social hierarchies are innate and likely evolved to support survival within group living. This seems logical, considering the early sapiens needed the support of a group and communicative skills with other tribes to survive. Leaders would speak to other leaders to make decisions, and we required a chain of command to pass along information to communicate effectively.

Many beliefs about power have been both beneficial and detrimental. War and conflict have taught us that world peace is nearly impossible, and working together to conserve the planet seems unreasonable. Regardless, in the twenty-first century, we find wisdom in the principles of a hierarchy—principles that form multiple practices for government and religion. Intentionally, the two concepts should construct the order to lead us toward discovery. This chapter focuses on the trajectory of progress parallel to material suffering throughout history and the narrative that influenced the perspective of existence. Use this chapter and its lessons to build an awareness of self. Throughout time, we see errors and the desire to manipulate material for the benefit of a few.

CULTURAL BELIEFS

Possibility in a realm beyond what we interpret is met with faith and a balanced structure. To express faith, we have developed beliefs around our culture. Cultural beliefs practice faith through religion and other ways to shape our character. Ranging from worldwide churches to spiritual traditions and local sects, it's hard to pinpoint the exact number of religions practiced globally today. There is no distinct beginning, and most understanding revolves around a theory of when and where religion began.

Researchers can date back thousands of years to ceremonial burials and writings on the wall, leading us to believe that early sapiens had faith in the afterlife. Abstract shapes and patterns etched into cave walls near presumed burials help guide modern-day anthropologists into the origins of religion. One theory is that tribes needed to expand from small groups to larger groups while maintaining order.

Survival was being scaled, and sharing standard value systems created attachment. The strength of the group belonged to the depth of these connections. As cohesive groups migrated out of Africa, the physical stress of travel and encounters with unfamiliar cultures drove the need for material and nonmaterial culture. This included religion, used to negotiate identities and relationships between groups. Information needed to be exchanged, and understanding authority allowed such transactions to coexist.

Without concrete evidence, hunter-gatherers most likely belonged to egalitarian societies and did not practice a defined religion. Hunter-gathers' governments related to one another as equals. Everyone was responsible for the health and development of the tribe. Without large-scale nations and city-states, the population was neither civilized nor big enough to require structured systems, such as an economy, health care, trade, or urban planning. However, the beginning of complex behavior favors the philosophy of egalitarianism and the practice of animism.

This indicates that animism was the world's first religion to focus on nature-based beliefs. Animism is the belief that all natural phenomena, including humans, animals, plants, rocks, lakes, and mountains, share one vital quality and a spirit that energizes them. This means humans are not the only ones capable of independent action; for example, a body of water is just as capable of rising to kill an unsuspecting person as a human enemy. In other words, all natural things were considered to carry a soul.

Maybe it was that defined gods and spirit ancestors were absent in the history of the earliest humans. Whether likely or not, the practice of animism can't be confirmed by our sapiens ancestors. However, it sparked cultural evolution and our start to religious practice, especially considering that the belief and connection humans share with nature still exists. Today, we see forms of animism practices such as Shinto, Hinduism, and Buddhism.

THE BIRTH OF RELIGION

A significant place to begin our understanding of religious practice emerges in shamanism as the fundamental trait of animism. Shamanism is regarded as one of the world's oldest religions and has evidence of shamanic practices belonging to Paleolithic cave art. It is suggested that animistic beliefs perked our faith in an afterlife while worshipping the spirits of all living things. In its footsteps was the creation of shamanism and ancestor worship, a fellowship needed to stabilize beliefs.

For this reason, shamans established personalistic relations with specific spirit beings, which paired well with rituals designed to commemorate the spirits of one's deceased forebears. These rituals helped structure the curricula needed for religion to continue. While fear gave substance to the afterlife, we created a stable structure teaching us how to live. We found wisdom from the deceased as their spirits walked us to our eternal home.

Ancestor worship dates to the Neolithic period and is one of the oldest elements of religious culture. With the belief that deceased family members have continued existence, the spirits of deceased ancestors will look after the family while taking an interest in the world's affairs. For example, a shaman is a practitioner who acts as a mediator to the spirits and is considered the "one who sees." This made the shamans spiritual men and women believed to be the visionary and spiritual intermediaries. They would communicate with the spirits on behalf of the community, including the spirits of the deceased, to find truth.

We've since dispersed as a species, developing unique traditions and cultures while creating our version of the original shamans. Therefore, the character who plays the "one who sees" across religions today is only diverse through a narrative.

AGRARIAN CULTURE

There may not be definitive evidence, but as far as we know, religion has been around as long as humans. This leads people of the twenty-first century into further confusion, wondering how much variation can belong to one concept that shares such similarity. We can take our curiosity to a point in history where physical exploration of Earth slowed down. The Americas were the final point of discovery as our ancestors crossed the land bridge of the Bering Sea. When early tribes made a final exploration from Asia to North America, it seemed the nomadic experience was ending. What came after the settlement was the structure of society and communities beginning to create their own story. Using supernatural spirits to guide the religious curriculum helped build the cultural hierarchy gripping the human experience.

As small tribes grew more extensive during the agricultural revolution 10,000 years ago, expansion was coined as agrarian culture. This meant that settlement and community-based tribes were now operating an economy based on producing and maintaining farmland. As the nomadic lifestyle died, our ancestors needed to cooperate and tolerate each other and nearby strangers. Once again, structure was created, and religion served as the perfect breeding ground to establish moral behavior. With time, sedentary existence allowed for the imagination to birth moralizing gods. From animism beliefs to shamanism and ancestor worship, the foundation was set to bring in higher deities. The transmission of religious concepts required complex thinking and the practice of mental imaging. This developed our consciousness and capacity for symbolic thinking as we communicated rituals.

The first agricultural civilizations developed around 3200 BCE during the Mesopotamia era, mainly in Egypt, Nubia, and the Indus Valley. Eventually, more would appear in China, Central America, and along the Andes Mountains of South America, nearing 2000-1000 BCE. These developments were a result of people creating more efficient systems of communication. As complexity in consciousness and population grew, order among each other seemed to remain a priority.

Religion and the government became the answer, and its structure enabled humans to create rules by following its laws. In this case, religion made sense as the scapegoat for who rules the ruler. Government leaders could quickly point to the skies to assure their people of the truth. Conforming to government law seemed logical if God was involved. Hence, the government needed religion as much as religion required the government.

CIVILIZATION STRUCTURED

Governments, gods, and structures developed as settling down around the globe allowed civilization to begin. Civilization was the social and cultural development stage that considered people the most advanced. Branches were put in place, allowing civilization both organization and meaning. For example, cities became microcosms of civilization and held tens of thousands of people. Towns were following, with thousands of people, and villages only had a few hundred people. A state is another branch of civilization consisting of several cities, villages, and surrounding farms.

States can reach millions of people and contain political, social, and economic hierarchies, including structure and degrees of power. For example, a hierarchy typically includes 10 percent of the people with the highest wealth and power over the remaining 90 percent. As states were built, those in power set the rules and accomplished order in various ways. Specifically, collecting taxes and tribute was often regarded as nonnegotiable from the top 10 percent. If necessary, the collections could even be gathered by force.

Imperial states eventually arose from the state's power, becoming known as empires. An empire was run by an emperor who stood as a single ruler and controlled the cities and farmland. In general, empires are created because of accumulating power and control. In Mesopotamia, powerful city-state rulers gained status by conquering their neighbors because power assured survival. As emperors survived and raised their status, they controlled the narrative. This means 90 percent of people living underneath the structure of power were most likely forced to perform the character they were assigned.

EMPIRES

The exercise of power dates to the first empire known as the Akkadian Empire of Mesopotamia (2330-2200 BCE), the first multinational political entity in the world. Sargon of Akkad took control of southern Mesopotamia in its first year of rule. Sargon solidified his control while pursuing several military campaigns to stabilize his power in Mesopotamia. His reach expanded from the Mediterranean Sea to the Persian Gulf, and his feats gathered control over much of the world at the time. The Empire developed culturally and commercially strong nations by conquering one city-state after another. At the time, the Sumer civilizations were known for language, governance, and architectural innovations. Believing in anthropomorphic polytheism, many gods were worshipped across each city-state.

Sumerians invented many technologies, including the wheel, mathematics, and script. With the acceleration in writing and telling time, consciousness multiplied in this area of the world. The momentum of inventions impacted society, and human advancement expanded our roles.

With relentless ambition and through a series of wars, Sargon conquered many Sumerian cities and controlled 30,000 square miles of territory in the making of one empire. The control awarded Sargon to influence the distribution of resources across the land and the religious perspective. As a ruler, he chose to preserve the Sumerian religion. However, he made the official language of Mesopotamia Akkadian.

In general, language transmits values, laws, and cultural norms. With the complexity of human language, structures are needed to control the direction. Like the sapiens sharing fictional stories around the campfire, early rulers knew communication influenced identity. If rulers could create boundaries of behavior, they could manage those living within their tribes. The success of the Akkadian Empire was its ability to control the language and behavior.

The rise of Sargon began with promoting trade within Mesopotamia and breaking down the physical and linguistic barriers. He used this strategy to unite his realm. For instance, the Akkadian Empire created the first postal system, where clay tablets inscribed in cuneiform Akkadian script were wrapped in outer clay envelopes marked with the name and address of the recipient and the seal of the sender. In a way, the address was used to track the population and maintain lines of communication. Collecting data and communicating it this way made it easier to correlate behavior.

The postal service made the most efficient use of bureaucracy at a larger scale. Metaphorically, Sargon was the first of our kind to narrate stories and influence behavior outside the campfire. He could scale communication to the point where we no longer needed to be physically present to communicate with one another.

The Empire held the region for a few hundred years and imprinted its philosophies among the people. As the collective consciousness grew, human perspectives allowed for the development of art, literature, and science. With its development, our species began to take mental imagery and symbolic thinking into heightened realms. We were becoming powerful in all aspects: cognitive, emotional, physical, and spiritual.

As the Empire grew, writing and religious practices infiltrated the customs of those they conquered. In Sargon's writing, he claimed that he had conquered "the four corners of the universe." This shows just how small the original empire was compared to the world today and how powerful control was in influencing beliefs. Similarities of supremacy between sapiens and emperors stand out in the ability to control the narrative. Storytelling around a fire expanded into large-scale conformity as trends exercised a more expansive range with our early rulers' beliefs. Power could now influence entire civilizations of people.

THE ROMAN EMPIRE

The Roman Empire is an example of such potency. At its height, it was the most extensive political and social structure in Western civilization. With impacts still apparent today, its roots were built upon the Roman republic—a form of government copied by countries for centuries.

The republic model allowed citizens to elect representatives to rule on their behalf. Citizenship varied, but one way Rome grew its empire was unique. Rome's approach to conquering lands was to rule those people as conquered subjects. They would invite those they conquered to become citizens, making people a part of Rome rather than enemies fighting against it. The new citizens would receive the same legal rights as everyone else.

Early Roman history was often a state of constant warfare. Surrounding neighbors were a persistent threat. Many conflicts arose during its tenure, specifically the three Punic Wars. Fighting the Carthaginians, Rome was nearly captured. The people of Carthage lived in modern-day Tunisia, Africa, and were a prosperous trading civilization. The land and trade began to conflict with the Romans. The two sides went on to fight three bloody wars (264-146 BCE) in pursuit of controlling the trade routes in the western Mediterranean Sea.

In the second war, Hannibal, a Carthaginian general, nearly succeeded in taking over Rome but could not conquer the city of Rome itself. Controlling much of modern-day Italy for over a decade, Hannibal was finally defeated by the Roman general Scipio at the Battle of Zama in 202 BCE. By the third and final war, Rome was able to end the threat for good. They burned the Carthage city to the ground and, according to stories, poured salt into the soil of their lands. This way, nothing could ever grow there again.

The Roman Empire survived, and the republic was safe. The Empire would become the world's largest and most influential political and military entity. This lasted nearly one thousand years, and over seventy emperors ruled until its end in the fifth century AD.

Initially, the Roman Empire was primarily a polytheistic civilization and worshipped multiple gods and goddesses. Over time, religious beliefs changed, and ripple effects began that impacted the soul of humanity today. The modern era and our world's most prominent religious practice is Christianity. Much of the religion's influence can be credited to the Roman Empire.

Nearing the end of the Empire, a pivotal moment occurred at the Battle of the Milvian Bridge in 312 AD—a significant battle in the Roman Civil War between Constantine I and Maxentius. Following the collapse of the Roman Empire's second tetrarchy, both rulers asserted competing claims to the imperial throne. As the story goes, Constantine and his army saw a cross of light in the sky above the sun with words in Greek that translated into Latin, In hoc signo vinces (In this sign conquer). Constantine, who practiced pagan monotheism then, attributed victory to the god of the Christians.

The night before victory, after seeing the sign in the sky, Constantine had a dream. In the dream, Christ directed him to use the sign of the cross against his enemies. Awakening from the dream, he marked his soldiers' shields with the Christian symbol. Following the victory, Constantine became a believing Christian who shifted his desire to promote the faith.

Before Constantine was the emperor, Diocletian, in 303 AD, began the last significant persecution of Christians in the Roman Empire. The result was the mass destruction of churches and the execution of Christians who refused to sacrifice to the Roman gods. However, in 313 AD, Constantine issued the Edict of Milan, which accepted Christianity. A decade later, Christianity became the official religion of the Roman Empire.

In 324 AD, Constantine was made master of the Roman Empire and became famously known for his connection to Christianity and the conversion of Rome. As the Empire ironed out theological disagreements among Christians from its past, priests were appointed to high office and given the same privileges as pagan ones.

Notable checkpoints solidified Christianity's presence across the Empire. For instance, the emperor personally attended the Council of Nicaea in 325 AD, intended to address the entire body of believers. Constantine died a few years later, in 337 AD. However, Christianity was well on its way to becoming the Empire's state religion.

Today, Rome is the center of unity and the beginning of the Catholic Church. Each subsequent emperor (except Julian the Apostate) ascribed to the Christian faith. Impressively, Theodosius I made Catholicism the official religion of the entire empire at the end of the fourth century. During the Middle Ages, the Catholic Church spread, and the Pope was the benchmark for Christian truths.

The Pope is the Bishop of Rome and is seen to have the supreme power of jurisdiction over the universal church. With this power, the Pope controls the matters of faith, morals, church disciplines, and government. The Pope's power bled into world affairs, which caused many people in surrounding tribes and nations to accept Catholic teachings. Today, the consensus of the Christian faith is around 2.4 billion followers.

INFLUENCE

Fighting each other for resources ever since leaving Africa, power has always maintained its demand. If it's the power we seek, hierarchy sustains that structure, and the characters that took the leap of faith to run the hierarchy have controlled our narratives. Whether through positive influences or corrupted manipulation, the storyteller at the campfire holds the attention of the material mind and body. Often creating the character for our experience, we quickly lose touch with the soul under the influence of material power.

Famous empires like the Mongol Empire were highlighted for conquering an enormous landmass during the thirteenth and fourteenth centuries. They are an example of mass domination and the lengths to which empires could influence narratives. The Mongol Empire was ruled by Genghis Khan, who is viewed by many as one of history's most outstanding leaders.

Styled as the "Universal Ruler," he and his empire were led by force. Known for leaving devastation in their path, committing acts of violence, and ruling by fear, entire cities asked for mercy—conquering much of the world en route to covering over 17 percent of the landmass and ruling a quarter of the world's population.

Driven by fear, the Mongols were relatively lenient regarding religious beliefs. Well known for warfare, the Empire was also celebrated for peace. When conquered, the Mongols exempted religious leaders from taxation and allowed the free practice of religion, whether it be Buddhism, Christianity, Taoism, or Islam. The idea ensured a more accessible governance of conquered territories. They felt their native religion and belief in shamanism did not need to be pressed upon those they conquered. Feeling this counterproductive, they sought to ingratiate themselves with the foreign cleric leaders to facilitate governance.

The Empire was technologically advanced and naturally relied on much land to sustain its farming and flocks. It provided the resources for goats, sheep, and horses, which depended on abundant grass and water. Genghis Khan also united Mongolia's tribes and supported China's peasant economy by controlling the taxes. He was able to build a structure that navigated rural cooperation, which formed the law of his people.

His power set the scene for military-feudal form, where the ruler offered fighters a unit of land to control in exchange for military service. If you were to accept the land, you would become a vassal, someone who swore loyalty and service to the superior ruler. Genghis Khan, who granted the land, could expand and influence quickly as a part of feudalism philosophy. His ideas behind religious freedom offered peace, and he embraced all trade routes to adopt the Empire's advanced technology. Establishing loyalty, warriors were rewarded and willing to fall in line with the Empire's vision, quickly becoming the most successful army of its time.

After powerful empires such as the Roman Empire or the Mongol Empire, we experienced the most recent and world's largest empire. Closest to us in time, the British Empire began in the sixteenth century and flourished as it grew dramatically until its demise in the twentieth century. The empire controlled nearly fourteen million square miles and 24 percent of the world.

The Empire shaped travel, the economy, technology, and politics. Persuasion far exceeded religious beliefs, and the Empire greatly influenced the world narrative. For example, the abolition of slavery occurred when Britain decided to abolish the international slave trade in 1807 and even outlawed it throughout its overseas territories in 1833. To many, this is one of the Empire's most important acts.

Many opposed the idea then and attempted to continue the trade, but the Empire's navy was too strong. They were able to control the oceans and water channels expressly set up to catch ships carrying slaves. It is most likely that most of these captures were those trying to get slaves across the sea and into the Americas, but the British Empire was able to put a stop to the movement. By the end of the nineteenth century, slavery was illegal in Europe and the Americas and eventually declared illegal throughout the world in 1948.

Another influential note on behalf of British rule is language. A positive byproduct of narrative control from the Empire was the spread of the English language. Today, it is the most prominent language in the world, making global communication much more accessible. It has allowed us to advance in science, law, navigation, and diplomacy. Building new roles for humanity, today, Britain is considered a motherland and a multicultural melting pot.

GOVERNMENT

According to the force theory, the government originated using force and coercion. As early city-states evolved, societies' most vital groups and potent individuals imposed their will on others. By establishing themselves as rulers, they could control the narrative of their lands. Government, in a peaceful sense, is to keep us safe, and those who are weaker than the most vital individuals or groups of people need the aid and support of the government to survive.

There are multiple forms of government practices around the world. The variety changes across cultures; however, they share many similarities, like religion. Each government provides parameters for the behavior of its citizens. They are put in place to protect them from outside threats and provide for their well-being. Undoubtedly, the structure of government to which an individual belongs will impact the character they play. It will carve the traditions and cultural practices of the citizens to the philosophy of their country's leaders.

In early city-states like Sumer, Kings ruled in the name of the gods they worshipped. Eventually, a single king, Sargon, created an empire and built the first monarchy, meaning there was one ruler—like a king, except the ruler of an empire covers many countries, while a king typically rules just one kingdom. Governments exercise a broader spectrum and focus on the political authority over specific actions within a nation, state, or community.

Governments today are viewed as a group of people who control and make the decisions regarding a specific country or state. Responsibilities are somewhat similar worldwide, but duties are executed differently depending on the form of government. The standard government structure is represented in a democracy, a republic, socialism, a dictatorship, communism, or a monarchy. To maintain order, most modern-day governments consist of executive, legislative, and judicial branches. Executive branches are in place to enforce the law. Legislative branches make the law, and judicial branches interpret the law.

Throughout history, while it seemed humans of power set the law, God was the source that looked over people and their welfare. The gods protected crops and cities while maintaining survival in agrarian culture. As the population grew, structure created changes due to complexity. Influential individuals needed to build empires and governments to manage the narrative. Communities were becoming too large, making sustaining order and following laws challenging. Cooperation with one another was under constant evaluation, and many times throughout history, the hierarchical power needed to take charge.

The constant adaptations to rising complexity forced the evolution of thinking and changed gods. For example, the change in perspective from pagan monotheism to Christianity with Constantine influenced the Roman Empire. Adjustments being made to spiritual beliefs created similar conflicts among communities. This makes the two intertwine marvelously as we study the influence of our character through government and gods.

The world has known many rulers and, therefore, many gods. Today, we practice five primary religions: Hinduism, Judaism, Buddhism, Christianity, and Islam. Ironically, all five religions emerged around the same time. Recognizing the influence and structures to maintain order, we used religion as aggressively as the government to control the narrative. The power dynamics of government and religion balance the uncertainty that anchors suffering, which makes it exceptionally easy for us to identify with an object and consider it valid. When the receptionist at a hotel believes they are the receptionist only, they lose the subjectiveness of nothing. When we think we are the government or religion, we, too, begin to justify ourselves. When we justify it on a large scale, our history has proven war. We can't debate with an open mind because, once again, we'd rather die defending our truth.

Ironically, the government needs religion to survive just as much as religion needs government. The issue occurs when we believe these structures solely identify life's meaning. Throughout history, our characters impetuously follow the material structure as truth, which creates imbalances between being and becoming. The more we understand how reality coexists, the deeper our relationship grows toward the soul.

UNITED STATES OF AMERICA

A country that has exploded in recent centuries through innovation, the United States is a tremendous case study regarding our connection with government and religion. Built on democracy, the power is vested in the people. The United States government is elected by citizens, and voting creates the hierarchy of officials. These officials are, in turn, held accountable to represent the citizens' ideas and concerns.

In the earliest stages of creating the structure within American history, the founding document of the Declaration of Independence points directly to the interconnectedness of government and religion. The Declaration of Independence states the principles on which the government and identity of the American people are based. As America defied the most powerful nation at the time to earn its freedom, it used the Declaration to legitimize its separation from Britain.

The American Revolutionary War, an epic political and military war that lasted from 1765 to 1783, saw the American colonies fight their way to freedom. During this time, they rejected the imperial rule of the British Empire. Protesting began in opposition to taxes that King George III required. The American colonies argued that taxation without representation in Parliament was unfair.

The American patriots led the revolution through battle, while the Founding Fathers severed political connections to Great Britain by signing a summarized Declaration seeking independence. Signed and delivered, the American colonies adopted the principles and stood tall as a developing country on July 4, 1776. The date remains the country's Independence Day; up to this point, the Declaration has stood independently without ever being amended.

The first ten amendments are called the Bill of Rights, and the First Amendment distinguishes them.

> *Congress shall make no law respecting an establishment of religion, or prohibiting the free exercise thereof; or abridging the freedom of speech, or of the press; or the right of the people peaceably to assemble, and to petition the Government for a redress of grievances.*
> —First Amendment

Religious freedom is a fundamental right in America and the first among rights guaranteed by the United States Declaration of Independence. It is the right to think, express, and act upon your beliefs. The document states that individuals have the right to practice their religion or not at all. The Founding Fathers had a theory that they would need to keep the government out of religion to protect religious liberty. The First Amendment, therefore, was created to sustain a separation between the church and the state.

Freedom was the incentive to become an American. The focus was creating a land of opportunity where all men are equal. Whether a person is European, Native American, or African, the new frontier promoted privilege. American citizens could access fundamental rights and speak freely while worshipping any God they choose.

Still, the freedom to worship different gods isn't much different from the Mongol Empire, which allowed those they captured to keep their religion. It's not drastically different from Constantine, who gently pushed Christianity to become the new religion in Rome. However, the country prided itself on being the most accessible country in the world. A philosophy birthed through liberation; however, its history is slightly misunderstood.

Americans began their progress by debating where to draw the line between religion and government since it was founded, and the separation created war and conflict among themselves. For instance, the early settlers captured indigenous people, made them slaves, and conquered their territories as they colonized the New World. Some of the Founding Fathers were slave owners themselves when they signed the Declaration of Independence. Much of the region's economy was shaped by slavery in the eighteenth century, and the Bible was often used to justify slavery as they reconciled with their decisions to keep the economy growing.

American freedom today still seems to be influenced by religious views. For example, the country debates whether it's unconstitutional to teach religion in school, and almost all presidents elected to run the country have been Christian. The Constitution requires federal officeholders to be sworn in on a sacred text, and God is referenced four times in the Declaration of Independence. The Liberty Bell, a symbol of freedom in the United States, has the inscription of a Bible verse from the King James Version—from "Leviticus 25:10"—"Proclaim Liberty Throughout All the Land Unto All the Inhabitants thereof."

The First Amendment clearly expresses separation between government and religion, yet the twenty-first century operates in harmony. In a country formed by colonies of people fleeing the British Empire, early settlers were influenced generationally by kings and emperors. This means their consciousness was bombarded with religious demands and forged through centuries of war. When the colonies won freedom from the British, they repeated what they knew.

REFLECTION

Without words, we must consider the influence of reality while learning to observe the state of being. If we are here to experience the third dimension through the lens of a human experience, we must come to terms with the characters needed to uphold society's standards. As we work together, the structure's push and pull impacts interpretation differently. Our unique perspective on the universal whole cannot be met in absolute agreement.

Therefore, the individual must play within the rules while bending the boundaries. Our character within the structure is an illusion of who we are; no hierarchical power can define that. We would need to move beyond the surface of illusion to comprehend the depth of our soul. This requires creativity and acceptance of nothingness from the individual playing a role in material reality. For that reason, ultimate power does not come from a structured hierarchy.

CHAPTER 5

PHILOSOPHY

As we study the mechanics of human nature, we seek to understand the philosophies that we've created. By examining the nature of reality, we can improve our structure. This chapter shifts to the philosophical approaches that guide our being within the human experience. In our pursuit of accurately suffering, we're given a narrative from natural and supernatural rulers. Philosophy helps us analyze concepts and enhance our problem-solving capacities. While we spend our lives organizing ideas and witnessing world issues, we aim to pursue questions of value and discover what is essential from the narration of the modern world.

As we seek guidance, we regularly pay attention to religion. Religion is derived from the Latin word *religare*, meaning *to bind together*. In other words, religion is a set of protocols that helps maintain the relationship between people and God. The definition is believing in the supreme power and worshipping this power as the creator and controller of the universe without reasoning. A higher power that we find value in because its structure takes rational thinking away from our being. Naturally, we create comfort by relinquishing the responsibility of thought to powers outside ourselves. This chapter aims to open the mind to a personal commitment to understanding oneself.

To most, religion is a human instrument and falls into two primary categories: Abrahamic religions, such as Christianity, Judaism, and Islam, or Indian religions, which include Hinduism, Buddhism, and Sikhism. Nearly 85 percent of the world identifies with a religion, while 1.1 billion consider themselves unaffiliated or atheist. Nonreligious practices are primarily seen in nations such as Estonia, the Czech Republic, China, and Japan.

Geographically, Estonia is a country in northern Europe, the Czech Republic is landlocked in central Europe, Japan is an island country in East Asia, and China is in Southeast Asia. Throughout history, powerful governments ruled Estonia and the Czech Republic, controlling the narrative and influencing their religious perspectives. Today, they are categorized as nonreligious solely due to their lack of sustainability in a defined practice. The Japanese religious tradition has collided with several components of practices from Shinto, Buddhism, and Confucianism. China is the world's second most populated country and is regarded as a one-party communist dictatorship. The Chinese government controls the freedom of religious practice for the citizens, which makes it hard to quantify the country's perspective on religion.

Beyond these areas of the world, religion dominates much of modern thinking. Depending on an individual's birthplace, the culture and traditions within the geographical location will likely imprint each being's worldview. Philosophy can be viewed as a universal understanding of human knowledge and wisdom. Therefore, our characters can develop a level of strength in knowing themselves, for themselves.

WISDOM

Up to this point, the focus has been placed on structure. With structure, our hierarchical needs are met, and our relationship with certainty is fulfilled, but we are still left with duality in the human experience. Philosophy can help us discover subjectiveness and how we make sense of the things we cannot see or touch. We've proven capable of creating curricula and power systems to maintain order, but to the individual seeking truth, how is it that we develop wisdom?

Philosophia—the love of wisdom—by definition, is a pursuit of becoming wise. It is the process of developing wisdom through intellectual search and logical reasoning. Philosophy has come to our way of understanding the world through questions. In many ways, this separates the human species from the animal kingdom. Specifically, in our way of thinking, humans can live a life with logic. The character's rationale lives within the conscious brain and is used to solve problems, make decisions, and generate creative ideas that develop material.

Human experience is a desire for truth; therefore, we must understand how to use philosophy to connect with the soul. Curating an ideology that detaches from the narration of our material world builds confidence in searching for what's worth pursuing in life. When our awareness can filter through material and act on our soul's intentions, we become wise.

PHILOSOPHY BACKGROUND

Questions we often find in philosophy come from our thirst for knowledge. Our curiosity is in a constant quest to gather information. In time, we pick up experiences and lessons that shape our perspective. Using philosophy to help turn events and knowledge into wisdom, when an individual becomes wise, they enhance their ability to think and form good judgment. Their actions are sound and provide insight into the world around them.

Improved communication and judgment are skills needed to enhance the well-being of consciousness. Our minds placed us at the top of the food chain and are ours to understand. Therefore, consciousness needs to study its psychology and behaviors by recognizing patterns. This is one of the ways we gain awareness and access to accepting subjective reality.

Our ancestors used the mind to control the world physically by overcoming threats from predators. Now we must use the mind to control the world mentally by overcoming spiritual threats. This evolution of consciousness is based on philosophy and forces our minds to remain flexible. As a result, consciousness experiences creativity, and we'll evolve the connection of our being to the state of becoming within our soul.

Wisdom dates to the sixth century BCE, when the first scientists of Western history began their pursuit of philosophy. The focus was Revolutionary theories concerning the natural world, human knowledge, and relationships with the gods. Within a few centuries, famous philosophers began to emerge. For instance, Socrates ignited the intellectual revolution that forever challenged traditional notions of our values and morality. The list goes on with his students, spotlighting Plato, who took philosophy down his own path with his discussions of logic, ethics, poetry, physics, and metaphysics. His work was combined with Aristotle's, and they are credited with birthed Stoicism, Epicureanism, and skeptical thinkers.

Another form is classical philosophy, which has influenced prominent figures such as Marcus Aurelius, Plotinus, Porphyry, and the fathers of early church life. For example, St. Augustine is one notable source who is recognized as a doctor of the church.

He was a Catholic bishop of Hippo (now Annaba, Algeria) and the first Christian philosopher in the fourth and fifth centuries AD.

These names stick throughout history because of their contributions to wisdom—contributions that help us discover the soul. Our souls are the state of becoming that intermediates between the mind and body performing materially. As our character changes roles throughout the material world, our soul is the gateway to further dimensions. Through teachings such as philosophy, we acquire information about certain truths that guide our souls. The philosopher focuses on shaping critical thinking to understand, making it a staple in our foundation for self-discovery.

HISTORY OF SCIENCE

The history of science is a somewhat academic discipline that covers many subjects. Its broad scope includes technology, mathematics, medicine, and astronomy. Science is our way of discovering what's in the universe. It's our way of seeking out how things work and figuring out what worked in the past and what could work in the future.

The ancient Greeks were the first mathematicians and scientists of the West. Examples of these early thinkers are Thales, Pythagoras, Empedocles, and Anaximander. They sought to make sense of the world by studying the evidence they found within it. Their curiosity led to many groundbreaking advances, and their foundation was the ability to question as they worked in the field of unknowns.

Thales declared that the first principle of all things is water—a life force that we recognize today as a necessity for survival. Thales believed Earth floated on the water, and Anaximander was under the idea that Earth was a solitary body. He thought we were floating free and unsupported in the universe and contributed to the world's first map. Empedocles believed the world acted upon forces of attraction and repulsion. His perspective was that the world consisted of diverse material elements. All matter is composed of four distinct elements: fire, air, water, and earth.

Uniquely, Pythagoras was an ancient Greek mathematician and philosopher. Today, we are familiar with his work because of the famous Pythagorean theorem, a mathematical formula for finding the length of the hypotenuse of a right triangle. His work recognizes the metaphysics of numbers and the conception of reality, including music and astronomy. He believed that our most profound level of math is in nature and used philosophy for spiritual purification to aid the development of a heavenly destiny. His teachings were organized around the possibility that our soul rises to unionize with the divine.

Overall, the Greeks used astronomy to develop ideas of mathematical science, a system used to study everything in the universe. Even beyond Earth's atmosphere, astronomy includes objects we can physically see, such as the sun, moon, planets, and stars. It's the oldest of the natural sciences and helps combine aspects of math and physics to study how the universe was formed.

Astronomy broke ground for several purposes, and many of its most essential usages sustained evolution and exist today. For example, our ancient Greeks were without GPS devices and traveled the world by land and sea. Using principles derived from astronomy, they positioned themselves and navigated by aligning with the stars. For instance, sailors and voyages used these tactics to explore unknown territories and develop the calendar to recognize the change of seasons. This improved trade routes and helped us explore the world. It also advanced our knowledge of seasonal patterns. Civilization knew when to plant crops and harvest efficiently, which allowed for settlement and safer travel.

The Greeks also advanced the field of medicine. They understood the body's nervous system and the nerve tissues within it. By inventing folk remedies and building case studies, they could, for example, patch up wounded gladiators. By dissecting how the body worked, they could perform surgeries and build recovery protocols for those who became sick or injured.

Furthermore, without using electricity or fossil fuels for energy, the Greeks built massive cities, sustaining millions of people. Their ability to advance science created conveniences and provided entertainment to keep the citizens of Rome happy. This part of evolution multiplied the options of characters the human experience could provide. Today, our gladiators create entertainment for our narratives worldwide, performing roles such as Olympian, American football, soccer, and hockey players. We build departments based on science to patch them up to keep the citizens of our nations happy.

PHILOSOPHY OF SCIENCE

Philosophy is a type of science that we use to understand things better. Branches include language, religion, and history. In a broad scope, we use the field of philosophy to explain what science is. We want to understand how things work and have logic behind knowledge.

Aristotle, a towering figure in ancient Greek philosophy, famously proclaimed, "Philosophy is the science of all sciences." He used function, classification, and hierarchy to build the foundation for explaining everything. We follow Aristotle's concepts daily, like how the world formed based on structure.

Today, modern science may see the world as a machine, whereas Aristotle saw it as an organism. Everything has a function or purpose, and its essential nature is to grow and achieve that purpose. He attempted to understand the whole universe, humanity, and culture as a working organism, which means everything applies to everything.

This idea of interconnectedness considers our ethics, politics, art, and connection to the natural world. Repeatedly, we are gripped by materialism within the mind and body and want one thing to be one thing. If we believe we are more than one thing or the character we play, we connect with the soul and experience the state of becoming in material reality.

Essentially, we would function daily with a sense of purpose. As discussed earlier, this is where we seem to be confused by material and spiritual suffering. To grow awareness, we must comprehend philosophy to bridge the gap between the states of being and becoming.

Here is a list of philosophy's main branches :

1. Metaphysics—study of the fundamental nature of reality.
2. Epistemology—study of the nature, origin, and limits of human knowledge.
3. Axiology—ethics, the study of what is right and wrong in human behavior, and aesthetics, the study of beauty and taste.
4. Logic—study of the nature and types of logic.
5. Political—study of government, addressing questions about the nature, scope, and legitimacy of public agents and institutions.

PHILOSOPHY OF METAPHYSICS : REALITY AND BEING

The branch of *metaphysics* deals with the first principle of things, including abstract things such as identity, time, and space. In many ways, the philosophy of reality and being is the desire and need to know, which gives us a place to start and study the character and soul through philosophy. For example, our need to understand reality weighs heavily on our minds, and through fear, we default to materialism. The abstract concept is overwhelming, and we repetitively can't break the chains of needing to know. We fail to ask questions without receiving an answer, which reiterates materialism. If we can detach from need, more profound questions receive the feeling from our soul.

Today, the modern use of metaphysics is the study of things outside objective measure. Think of God as the being, making God a metaphysical subject. We perceive God as the source of perfection and give answers to what that is. Since we can't interpret reality similarly, our answers are nothing more than a feeling. Therefore, we often debate our subjective feelings toward the topic of God as truth. If we consider God the ultimate being, we can only study what we believe God is; we cannot know God.

QUESTIONS TO PONDER :

What is consciousness?
Why is there something rather than nothing?

There is no need to answer the questions correctly. They only serve as a platform for exploration. For example, the objective answer for consciousness is the connection of our conscious, subconscious, and unconscious minds. We make decisions, form judgments, and plan with our conscious mind. We display our habits, experience emotions, and host long-term memory in our subconscious. Automatic functions within the body, such as breathing and immune response, are in our unconscious. These answers are reasonable and backed with objective measures, but what is consciousness?

We see the material world with our eyes, touch rocks, and swim in water. These are tangible signs that reality is objective.

This may be true, but go deeper and think of a rock. We can touch and see a rock, but how do we know it's real? Composed of crystals and minerals that fused together into a solid, without ever knowing when and how the crystals and minerals formed in the first place. In time, natural processes glued the crystals and minerals into a rock. We can see and touch the rock, which makes it real. The issue is that something had to come from nothing to form the rock, but what is nothing? This leads to the last question: why is there something rather than nothing?

Without words, our minds force everything into the material because we can't accept something as nothing. Therefore, we classify to assume that the rock is natural and explain its function, but we cannot say what it is. Similarly, as we explain consciousness, we cannot explain what it is. We repetitively make this mistake when speaking the truth materially. As we explain functions objectively, we can trust we are the character, but we cannot explain what that is. Through the philosophy of metaphysics, we study material while accepting the nothingness of reality.

PHILOSOPHY OF EPISTEMOLOGY : KNOWLEDGE AND TRUTH

Ancient wisdom tells us knowledge is power. To increase power and exercise control, we need to become thinkers who know about reality and being. The branch of *epistemology* takes this further by examining our knowledge and what we think is true. By exploring the limits of human cognition, two key contributions reside in rationalism and empiricism.

Rationalism is how humans comprehend knowledge through reason, while empiricism claims all knowledge comes through experience. When considering the differences, we ponder whether we can teach or acquire knowledge through experience.

The issue is familiar because we must have both to fully express ourselves. We need to study the knowledge given to us and experience it—the same as playing our being and remaining aware of becoming. Think of the character retaining information and the soul experiencing it.

While we attempt to expand this philosophy, we must acknowledge the perspectives our characters learn from. The better we communicate with each other, the more advancement in material truth and knowledge we can gather for the experience of our souls.

Our character receives knowledge through three concepts: dogmatism, agnosticism, and skepticism.

KNOWLEDGE AND TRUTH : EXAMINATION OF CHARACTER

Dogmatism—the concept that we can know the world fully. There is an avoidance from accepting others' beliefs, ideas, and behaviors.

Agnosticism—the concept that we are severely limited and cannot understand the world fully. It is a view or belief that God is unknown or unknowable.

Skepticism—the concept that gives us the medium and sees both sides. Neither positive nor negative. This is being doubtful and in an uncertain state of disposition.

As you can see, these are three different perspectives to examine. Studying the mind and becoming aware of how you examine the world is valuable. When we track progress in the material world, we create empirical evidence to expand the limits of these concepts. Rather than debate our own perspective, we can lean toward objective truths to settle arguments. This allows us to implement material knowledge into existence to adapt to the whole.

Since we can change what we measure, using scientific methods to keep our minds open without learning only one way is valuable. For example, as the Romans expanded thinking through science, they evolved their health practices. Evolution provided entertainment for their people and brought happiness to the human experience. The more we acquire knowledge from an open mind, the more we can invent such conveniences to make life easier.

Convenience awards time in the material world to spend with the soul and incentivizes us to keep learning. A modern example is our technical advancements, such as the cell phone. We have instant access to ask the internet questions and get immediate solutions. With its convenience, we no longer must study subjects to get answers. The cell phone is magical for this reason; however, the paradox is that it disrupts our process of acquiring knowledge through experience. It may be a convenience, but the issue and need for the philosophy of epistemology is to help us regain awareness of rationalism and empiricism. In this example, speed disrupted experience for the modern human.

The information era of the twenty-first century inundated us with too much knowledge, and as a cost, we've lost our depth. For instance, currently, two-thirds of the American adult population is obese. Yet we have a health industry that provides knowledge and creates baselines, such as temperature, heart rate, and blood pressure, to prescribe diets and lifestyle habits to sustain vitality. In theory, this should be one of history's most incredible advancements in health, but it does the opposite. The need to consciously think was delegated to an industry, and without proper experience, over two-thirds of the population became obese.

Each human living today carries with them a subjective opinion of the world. Dogmatic views on religion create wars and deny acceptance of others. Agnostic views carry an attitude lacking evidence, and skeptics often remain doubtful of possibility. We play these characters, and whether it be reason or experience, we see the world differently. As we shape philosophy around knowledge, it is crucial we take our time to figure out what we believe is true. The human desire for answers in the twenty-first century has been accommodated at such speed that we're often left materially suffering. The false perspective that we can have an answer within moments detaches us from our soul's experience as the character.

PHILOSOPHY OF AXIOLOGY : ETHICS AND AESTHETICS

Defined as moral philosophy, the branch of *ethics* is one of the most central disciplines of the field. Its focus is solely on what is morally good or bad. From the perspective of righteous living, the philosophy of ethics is based on how we should live in harmony with nature and our surroundings.

QUESTIONS TO PONDER

How do we live a meaningful life?
What is modesty?

Our ethics are based on how we act or behave to live a virtuous life. Intending to live a happy and focused life, most philosophers believe these answers belong to a simple and modest lifestyle.

Three Forms of Ethics
1. Meta-ethics—study of nature and the meaning of

moral statements.
2. Normative ethics—practicing and determining the moral course of action.
3. Applied ethics—within a specific and real-world situation, how should a human behave, and how should they focus their attention?

To survive, humans need to create boundaries of what is right and what is wrong. Good and bad behavior is considered our morality and the values and principles we conduct. As world order contains the boundaries of human morals, the study of ethics gives us perspective on right and wrong. Whether in small tribes or citizens of a country, we need structure to survive because it keeps organization among each other. Whether we receive our laws from religion or government, ethics is the goal in promoting the correct behaviors.

Meta-ethics wants to know what morality is and studies the nature of human behavior based on individual and societal morals. Philosophers study this concept not by resolving moral disputes but rather by answering questions. Should we all follow a set of moral principles, or do different principles apply to people in different cultures?

Normative ethics is more involved with how people should act. It focuses on the virtues an individual should have while emphasizing the importance of moral rules. If one is to break morals and display poor behavior based on the value system provided, there should be an emphasis on the importance of consequences for such actions.

Applied ethics is how we work through controversial topics or issues and determine what is right. Complex moral questions often arise as we try to figure out cooperation, especially with large-scale civilizations that exercise the power of government. For example, the United States' Second Amendment states, "A well regulated Militia, being necessary to the security of a free State, the right of the people to keep and bear Arms, shall not be infringed." It establishes that the government cannot infringe on the right, as an American citizen, to arm yourself. Therefore, we ask, *is it ethical that all citizens should have the right to bear arms?*

AESTHETICS

By studying the sense of beauty, we practice the branch of *aesthetics*. The philosophy is focused on the study of the arts. The intentions have a lot to do with an individual's taste and beliefs. Collectively, humanity shares consciousness as one. This does not mean we are equal in the sense of mind, body, and spirit. We all have a unique blueprint within the cosmos; however, we exist on the same planet with a degree of consciousness. Therefore, we can argue we are the same but vary with unique qualities.

Art is an expression and application of producing works from a consciousness that we do collectively and individually. Our art impacts society's narratives, meaning art influences the material world through the soul. It is one way we express subjectivity in the human experience.

QUESTIONS TO PONDER

Does beauty belong to the eyes of the beholder, or is there a standard and expectation for what we consider good and bad art?
Is art made by humans, or is it only found in nature?

Three Forms of Aesthetics
1. Imitationalism—the belief that art should look lifelike and focus on realistic representation.
2. Formalism—composition is the most critical aspect of art, and the emphasis is on the design qualities.

3. Emotionalism—art must create an emotional response from the viewer. The art is about the content.

Imitationalism is a theory of art that judges the work based on how realistic it is. The subject matter is portrayed as realistically as possible in categories such as portraits, statues, and photorealism. The judgment of work is based on how real the viewer perceives it, whereas formalism boosts the support of abstract art. The focus is on the artist's skills to perfect technique without consideration for context. The judgment of work is based on how the artist used lines, form, and composition. Emotionalism is how it sounds. Does the artwork communicate moods, feelings, and ideas to the viewer? For example, if a painting of nature promotes tranquility, the judgment is based on how successful the art communicates an emotional reaction from the viewer.

Since ancient times, humans have created art. It is the common language among humanity and something we all hope to understand. What separates it from what we know is that art is subjective, which makes it our way of expressing the soul to the material world. Therefore, philosophy is essential to examine and valuable for an individual to improve. Art is our way of communicating without words.

PHILOSOPHY OF LOGIC : ARGUMENTATION AND REASON

The study of correct reasoning is the scope and nature of *logic* philosophy. It contains both formal and informal logic. Logical thinking cannot involve emotions or mysticism. The focus must remain within a reasonable and rational framework. The focus should be on how to fit ideas together reasonably. The system should allow a person to investigate, classify, and evaluate the good and bad forms of reason.

Four Forms of Logic
1. Informal—the use of deductive and inductive reasoning to make arguments.
2. Formal—the use of syllogisms to make inferences.
3. Symbolic—the use of symbols to map out valid and invalid arguments.
4. Mathematical—the use of mathematical equations to prove theoretical arguments.

Argumentation and reason are ways in which we improve our thinking. Informal logic seeks to provide guidance to arguers in hopes of enabling them to argue more reasonably, avoiding fallacies and achieving success in persuasion. Well-reasoned argumentation improves reasoning skills while making sense of the world.

The difference between deductive and inductive is that deductive reasoning begins with a theory, supports it with observation, and arrives at confirmation. Inductive reasoning starts with observation, supports it with patterns, and arrives at a hypothesis. Inductive makes broad generalizations based on trends, compared to deductive reasoning, which begins with facts and deduces facts from others to find truth. For example, when scientists estimate the world's population, they are studying trends and forming an idea of when the population will be at eight billion people. The reasoning is generalized and based on the growth seen over the years.

Formal logic is founded on principles and philosophies. Informal logic often establishes the ground for formal logic, which makes them credible to each other. However, formal logic should be clear and conclusive. The statements are noncontradiction, meaning a statement can't be accurate and false simultaneously. The logic eliminates the middle and cuts to the result.

Symbolic logic represents logical expressions using symbols and variables instead of natural language. The goal is to prevent confusion by teaching incorrect reasoning, recognizing fallacies, and confirming the soundness of arguments. For example, in algebra, X represents a number. The symbol gives no clue as to the number's value; however, it is used to form sums and products.

The fourth form of logic is math. We often consider math and philosophy two separate subjects, but they are relatively similar. Many philosophers throughout history have been phenomenal mathematicians and believe it is required for thinking on an abstract level. To the ancient Greeks, for example, geometry was seen as the highest form of mathematics and formed the models for philosophy. For instance, logical learning with math enables a person to analyze cause-and-effect relationships and improve reason. Therefore, math allows us to learn using numbers and abstract visual information to form a clearer perspective of reality. With logical improvement, we can establish the roadmap for our characters as we set the stage for our evolving soul. Together, they form the blend of the human experience.

POLITICAL PHILOSOPHY : THE STATE AND GOVERNMENT

Political philosophy is a reflective process of arranging our collective life and forming a community. This philosophy's fundamental questions and focus are the state, government, liberty, justice, politics, and law enforcement. Political philosophy looks at the more profound and broader issues that exist within human structure. It is another way to view the meanings of political action and motivation.

QUESTIONS TO PONDER

What is political change?
What does it mean to preserve political power?
What does it mean to change political power?

All of this is dependent on the idea of "good." The idea that all those involved in politics are guided by an ethical sense of what they believe is good is derived from everything studied previously, including the nature of reality, knowledge, moral behavior, and logic.

We are now looking into the philosophy of powers that govern humanity. Humans have long debated their sides of opinion and often create conflict with the opposition. This happens because both parties try to argue their points about what they believe is good. This is expected behavior among our characters in the material world.

QUESTION TO PONDER

What is good?

The question has been dealt with throughout history, and we still debate it to this day. Political parties change often, and organizations and government policies shift. As time moves forward, our consciousness evolves through different perspectives. Keeping the structure of the moral code in mind and forming solid questions about societal changes helps us broaden our scope of reality. This allows us to acquire wisdom as a species with the ever-developing knowledge we provide to each other. Finding out what is good, from the perspective of an individual to the whole, is an infinite exploration into the soul of humanity. The issue happens when we believe we know or have found the truth. Typically, this leads to radical belief in a position, and as previously stated, we'll fight wars defending our image.

CHAPTER 6

PHILOSOPHY OF RELIGION

"Religion is regarded by the common people as true, by the wise as false, and by the rulers as useful."

—*Seneca*

We use philosophy to extract what is essential for our material lives. It helps us analyze concepts, arguments, and problems we encounter. This makes questioning religion crucial for the development of our characters. The sheer size of the religious impact on human evolution deserves its own study section. As we deepen our awareness of the framework of religion with a broad and narrow focus, we strengthen the apprehension of our characters.

Philosophy differs from religion in that no supreme creator exists, and we do not worship a god. Criticizing beliefs, philosophy looks for rational explanations and justifications for them. When we study religion, we recognize its attempt to offer a view of life and a sense of purpose behind the most basic and essential questions. However, religion's answers are not subject to the scrutiny of reason. Philosophy inveighs against its systems, severely examining everything and looking for logic.

Philosophy does not set out to eliminate religion. More so, critically think about religion and all its aspects. The focus centers around wonder and the importance of religion to create reason behind questioning it. The philosophy of religion should not be the perspective that we seek to destroy or alienate people from their faith. The observation and open mind to ask questions around a diverse practice that nearly 85 percent of the globe's population identifies with accounts for our intentions to understand. When we can freely question religion with the intent to grow knowledge, we allow wisdom to impact our souls. Fear of entering the realm of philosophy around religious diversity stunts that evolution.

Our psychological wiring operates to fulfill the needs of rationality, and logic may expose religious beliefs as inconsistent in various ways. This makes it frightening for the mind to investigate because we would rather know what we know than learn what we don't. Often, religion serves as the ultimate truth and requires no curiosity.

Developing a philosophy around religion gives power to the individual—opening communication to one's soul in pursuit of learning about the divine. Philosophy may find religion without evidence, even contradictory, but it does not attempt to disprove it. The aim is to reveal religious beliefs as beliefs rather than empirical claims. This allows religion the ability to create language that does not need to be scientific, and philosophy can help us accept such concepts.

It is helpful to be curious about religions because thousands exist. With various views of the world, we differ in how we live.

Therefore, we must ask questions while maintaining tolerance for cultures carrying diverse perspectives.

Here are a few common approaches to better grasp humanity's religious practices.

1. Atheism—the philosophy is to acknowledge the variety of different perspectives and consider them all to be wrong.
2. Agnosticism—this philosophy says, "I don't know." This point of view recognizes the world's religions and acknowledges that one doesn't know enough to believe in any of them.
3. Religious exclusivism—a philosophy that excludes all religions, believing only one religion is correct and all others are wrong and misguided.
4. Religious inclusivism—the belief that only one religion is entirely correct, but other faiths are partially true. It is often held by an individual who practices a specific religion and believes that to be the answer yet accepts that others exist.
5. Religious relativism—a philosophical stance that asks, "Who knows what is true?" An individual believes each religion can be considered true for its believers. It may not be true for them, but it can be true for you. Acknowledging everyone has different experiences, there's no objective way to discuss whether religious beliefs are true or false.
6. Religious pluralism—a philosophy with the stance that all religions are true. This perspective does not say all religions are true because they work for someone; instead, it states all religions are objectively true because they are true. Religious diversity expresses the truth in different languages because of various cultures. We can practice religious pluralism in two ways: all religions say

the same thing about reality but speak it differently, or all religions are true, saying different things to prescribe solutions to various problems.

The framework of these approaches helps navigate how our characters perceive material religion. Since we're searching for answers in the religious quest, individuals often deplete their tolerance for recognizing and respecting the beliefs and practices of others. Only a curiosity about understanding the world's ways offers an opportunity to shift attitudes.

With wisdom from the soul, perspective can shift from rejecting to understanding religious views. We can question how certain cultures developed structures for their civilizations to survive. Each community was aware of the afterlife, and in our need for meaning, connecting with a god served a purpose. Exercising patience does not affirm everyone is right. Instead, it realizes everyone is significant. This opens the channels to collective understanding and clarifies the unique characters worldwide.

QUESTIONS TO PONDER

Can someone hold exclusivism or inclusivism while also maintaining tolerance?
Why could relativism and pluralism not lead to religious empathy?
Should we strive for religious tolerance?

Religious disputes have led to horrific acts of violence for centuries. In the name of faith, people are influenced dramatically. We believe religion controls our lives and gives us the certainty we need. To understand the character, we must think about beliefs and how we got them, considering sacred texts and how they were written. Religion is a system that points to the world beyond, and our souls seek practices that center around the transcendent. In the material world, utilizing a philosophical approach to religion broadens intelligence to cultural interpretation.

WORLD HISTORY PHILOSOPHIES

What makes the world unique are its individuals. We carry qualities that serve the greater good. Whether we're justified in our actions or not, our contribution to society is needed to continue the evolution of consciousness. We move the needle in evolution by tapping into our souls. The more we comprehend the dualities of our character and expand that into overall awareness, the more we display our powers.

Religion guides thought with an immaculate creator, and philosophy grants wisdom. These wisdoms support the behaviors of our world and what we deem right from wrong. Studying the world teaches us to step back from our daily thinking. We begin to explore awareness and ask the questions that underpin our thoughts. We become capable of articulating our own arguments.

As we grow tolerance with religious practices, hierarchical powers, and structure, we develop composure for ourselves. Constant refinement of the self sharpens morals and behaviors by controlling one's emotions, enabling stability for life's harshness. Therefore, studying philosophy enhances a person's ability to contribute to organized thought. As a byproduct, we intentionally move through life dealing with questions of value and extracting what is essential from the world's material. We form our own worldview and understand the opinions of others. In a transformation of maturity, we become balanced.

Through organized thinking, we've curated teachings that bind us together, like religion, such as Stoicism, Confucianism, and Taoism. As we study these three doctrines, what makes them unique is their consideration of religion. They are sparked from consciousness and, for many cultures, evolved into religious practice. To this day, the concepts exist, and depending on perspective, the ideology can be both a philosophy and religion. This makes the practices valuable to ponder because they were birthed in the material world without a supreme creator.

STOICISM

Stoicism was one of the dominant philosophies during the Hellenistic period—a period referring to all the ancient territories that were influenced by Greek culture after Alexander the Great's conquests and during the rise of the Roman Empire.

Alexander the Great was one of world history's greatest military strategists and leaders. He was ruthless and dictatorial and even considered himself divine. His ambition led him to the position of king, starting in 336 BCE, but he would die thirteen years later, which began the Hellenistic period. During his tenure, Alexander built an empire that stretched from Greece to India, an empire-building campaign that would change the world and spread Greek ideas from the Eastern Mediterranean to Asia.

Rome, however, was an empire whose culture was depraved, and corruption was a significant problem toward the end of the Empire. In the developmental years of Stoicism, the teachings of moral behavior were popular to many because of the Empire's depravity. According to stories, the first generation of Stoic philosophers congregated and lectured within the walls of Athens and originated as a Hellenistic philosophy. Lessons were taught to corral the behavior and morals of the people of Rome.

The philosophy was founded by Zeno of Citium around 300 BCE and would be passed down for generations. Life became troubled when the power game took over in Greek city-states from Hellenistic kings who succeeded Alexander. The insecure environment built two dogmatic philosophical systems: Stoicism and Epicureanism.

The intentions were to give their adherents something to make them independent of the external world. Zeno's thought essentially stated that the basis of human happiness is to live "in agreement" with oneself. Later, the statement was replaced by the formula "to live in agreement with nature." By living in agreement with nature, a human being has virtue.

The idea was to give power to the individual and guide them with self-control during turbulence. For instance, wealth, poverty, health, and illness concepts were considered indifferent. Life and death were considered indifferent as well, and the sole focus of the practice was to exercise Stoic control over your being in the material world. The virtues were intended to practice proper knowledge by exercising self-awareness and choice. Everyone was expected to have fortitude in knowing what must be endured and what must not.

The Stoic schools of thought developed Zeno's philosophy and even became the religion of republican opposition during the Roman Empire. As the republic collapsed, Stoicism became the philosophy of choice for Roman elites who had lost their roles in governing the republic and could only rule the "inner empire" of their souls.

The movement created a philosophy of collaboration rather than a religion. It was viewed as a way of living, and Stoics used the principles to guide actions. In a call for help, the standard of living provided a compass directing people down the right path. The practice teaches four essential virtues.

Stoicism's Four Essential Virtues: Principles
1. Justice
2. Wisdom
3. Courage
4. Temperance

Justice is focused on fairness, kindness, and treating everyone with respect. Being aware of your place within society can create harmony and balance within communities. Justice is a moral compass and should focus on improving all. Marcus Aurelius wrote, "That what is not good for the beehive cannot be good for the bees."

Wisdom is focused on understanding the world around us and being able to see it for what it is. Individuals should be able to push aside their judgments, preconceptions, and prejudices to see reality as it is. Wisdom allows people to make sound decisions and recognize the difference between what everyone can control and what they cannot. As a result, our character learns from experiences, reflecting on actions and using awareness to navigate life's challenges.

The Stoics believed wisdom divided life into three categories: good, bad, and indifferent. Good is acting with virtue, bad is acting not virtuous, and indifference comes from all things we can use for good or bad. For example, the Stoics were indifferent toward money, possession, and fame, existing in the middle of good and evil because the result of indifference was due to an individual's awareness of the material world. If a character was materially suffering, they most likely used resources such as money and fame to corrupt decision-making, whereas the opposite may take place with a character spiritually suffering. They could use money and fame to advance the narratives of society to live a life of virtue.

In times of trouble, the Roman leaders of Stoicism needed faith to establish structure. In their minds, being the opposite of cowardice was courageous. Individuals could showcase courage in times of fear, desire, and anxiety. Stoicism believes in standing up for what is right by facing difficult situations and overcoming adversity without being overwhelmed by uncertainty. The sustainability in character was to stay true to principles in the face of unpopular or difficult things.

Stoics' final virtue was temperance. Seneca wrote, "So-called pleasures, when they go beyond a certain limit, are but punishments." This quote is an example of moderation. As the Roman Empire expanded its resources and gathered forms of entertainment for pleasure, individuals needed to maintain self-restraint, discipline, and control.

The era's characters needed to learn moderation by finding harmony in their advancing world. Progress provided money and fame, which drove characters into greed. The Stoics wanted to teach avoidance of excess while seeking simplicity. A philosophy established thousands of years ago rings true today, as we've only created more convenience and excess in the modern era.

CONFUCIANISM

Confucianism is a philosophy with the golden rule, "Do not do unto others what you would not want others to do unto you," which is another point in history where our characters were learning how to handle advancement and convenience. In the eastern part of our globe, China is a region that was born along two great rivers: the Yellow and Yangtze Rivers. People began farming and settling on the land roughly around 8,000 BCE and were ruled by small and decentralized dynasties.

The first known dynasty, the Xia dynasty, is thought to have existed from around 2070 BCE until 1600 BCE. In a mythical period, the first Xia king, Yu, was known for repairing damage caused by significant floods disrupting life. Yu fixed the issues and achieved the Mandate of Heaven, which is the divine right to rule. Power established hierarchy in the region, and the Xia dynasty built the foundation with familiar succession. This meant sons would follow their fathers to the throne.

Sooner or later, the Shang dynasty overthrew the Xia dynasty, which maintained control for nearly 600 years. This opened the region to structural and economic stability, allowing Chinese culture to flourish. The invention of writing was most notable in what historians consider the "golden age." In its wake, another longest-lasting dynasty was established when the Zhou king eventually overthrew the Shang king.

China's most influential writers and philosophers emerged during this period. Like in other areas worldwide, Greek conflict created Socrates's emergence, while competing kingdoms of India brought us Buddha. In search of truth and human morality, China experienced Confucius. Troubled times brought new ideas, as Confucius, a teacher and philosopher from 551 BCE to 479 BCE, wrote about good behaviors and ethics.

Immediately following his death, the "Warring States" period began, during which various regions of China started fighting. The Qin armies emerged victorious in 256 BCE, and Qin Shin Huang established the first empire. As history repeats, the ruler in the position of emperor controlled the narrative.

When dynasties shifted to Chinese unification, the surrounding territories were brought under the rule of Qin Shin Huang. He sought to standardize numerous aspects of life, such as coinage and the writing system. His administrative structure has served as a model for government in China to the present day. Although his empire was short-lived, only lasting fifteen years, it has influenced two thousand years of Chinese history.

In its path was the next golden age, a period in which Confucianism spread. The Han dynasty (206 BCE–220 CE) marked an era when the Silk Road was built, and trade routes were created from Asia to the Mediterranean and East Africa. The expansion allowed commerce to flourish, and writing became essential for communication. As a result, Confucianism became the official state religion.

Before Confucianism influenced the lands, emperors and leaders influenced the narrative with a concept called legalism. The concept presupposed that humans are fundamentally evil, which justified leaders exercising in terms of strict laws and harsh punishment. Confucianism came at the right time for the advancement of the region's spiritual suffering since the material world presumed all humans were driven by self-interest. Since the region believed this to be accurate, the intention of the structure was to be controlled by a strong ruler. As a result, strict laws were established, and the ruler was viewed as all-powerful.

Confucianism opposed these beliefs and relied on the fundamental goodness of human beings. Its practice aimed to restore order in a world falling apart. To do this, Confucianism created a system of five hierarchical relationships. In all five areas, the younger partner was expected to respect and honor the older.

IN ORDER :

1. Ruler to subject
2. Husband to wife
3. Father to son
4. Elder brother to younger brother
5. Friend to friend

Confucius believed the ruler set the example for everyone else. Therefore, it was the government's responsibility to uphold the highest standards of benevolence, meaning the quality of well-being and kindness came from the top down. Confucianism became a practice in ancestor worship, and human-centered virtues were essential for a peaceful life.

Known as a philosophy, Confucius thinking was grouped with religion but differed by not having an organized curriculum.

Although Confucius was confused between the two, he had a strong sense of reverence toward the heavens, which is not distinguishable from reverence toward life. For instance, a person must have a reverence for life and acknowledge heaven as the source of life. Therefore, existence is both material and divine.

Whether a philosophy or religion, Confucianism does not begin with Confucius. He was not the founder of the practice compared to Buddha, the founder of Buddhism. Confucianism is a set of beliefs that originated in Ancient China that variously describes the tradition, philosophy, religion, and theory of government as the way of life. Confucius exerted an influence on spiritual and political life only through his writings and recordings.

THREE ESSENTIAL VALUES IN CONFUCIANISM

> **Filial piety (Xiao)**—considered the most fundamental of the Confucian values and the root of all others. Promising to one's parents to respect and follow their orders.
> **Humaneness (Ren)**—consider the goal and the larger vision. Do not do unto others what you do not wish done to yourself.
> **Ritual (Li)**—the proper way of doing things in the most profound sense.

Filial piety is the root of Confucius's practice. The most important relationship is between the parent and their children. Parents are to provide the best care possible for their children by making sure they're safe and capable of growing. In return, the children must grow up and eventually take care of the aging parent as they once did for them.

Humanness is the care and concern for other human beings. A person who desires themselves to succeed helps others to succeed. This can translate to kindness because we need to care for ourselves to support those around us. If we follow our role and act with benevolence, order will be sustainable and work perfectly.

Ritual represents the form in which human action is supposed to take. Ritual allows for understanding relationships by performing ancestor worship and knowing filial piety is eternal. With this belief, children can continue to be loyal and obedient to their parents forever. At the same time, with worship, parents can continue teaching and serving the material world through their spirits.

TAOISM

Taoism, also known as Daoism, is traditionally said to have been founded between the sixth and fifth century BCE. The Dao or "the way" symbol contains three strokes. The first stroke represents balance, which is considered yin and yang. The middle stroke represents oneself, meaning Dao is within you. The third stroke means to move and act. Think of the symbolism representing the state of being while knowing the source of becoming is within you.

As a person spiritually experiences the material world through the characters they play, the individual is connected to the source as they move and act. Through our actions, we can find balance without an external god to rely on—a practice perceived as philosophy and religion, like Confucianism. The concept is that humans and animals live in balance with the Tao, and the spirit of the body will join the universe in the afterlife.

Tao Te Ching is the foundational text, a collection of poetry and sayings that guide the Taoist way of thinking and acting. Seen as the sacred text, Lao Tzu is the author and philosopher behind the concepts. There is little evidence, however, that he existed at all, and the book *Tao Te Ching* was written by many authors. Regardless, the practice recognizes Lao Tzu as the image of Tao.

The Tao is considered the source of reality. While creating an endlessly diverse universe, Taoists say human character is carved up by language, forced morality, and selfishness. Therefore, it's essential to see and feel within nature. The idea is that the whole human has infinite potential but is influenced by the environment. To thrive, you must stand outside the stream of life and live in the stream of nature by knowing you are the stream. This is the Taoist way of directing one's path from material to spiritual suffering.

When our being spiritually suffers, we experience what's called "Wu wei," a state of natural flow where actions become effortless. Flow is the path to enlightenment, and Taoism guides the living to be in a state of harmony with the universe. Chi, or qi, is the energy that presents this power, and to the Taoists, this energy is not a god; instead, gods are part of the energy. This means the gods are just like all living things, and flow balances the forces of duality. Yin and yang represent the matching pairs of the material world, such as hot and cold, light and dark, action and inaction. These opposites are needed for a universal whole because nothing can make sense by itself, hence the need for duality.

Taoism has been prominent in the eastern part of the world for centuries. Seeking enlightenment as the ultimate expression, one must become utterly free from worldly interests and passionate desires to reach happiness and supreme good. The law of unity by two opposite forces, yin and yang, teaches us how to connect with the soul. For example, if a person were to try too hard to attain a particular desire, the law of reversed effort would operate as a result, and the effect would be the exact opposite of what the person desired.

THREE PILLARS OF PRACTICE

Simplicity—a form of inaction (Wu wei) is the practice of not taking any action not in accordance with the natural course of the universe.
Patience—with friends and enemies. Admit your faults and mistakes.
Compassion—living in harmony with nature and always competing in a spirit of play to stay in harmony with the Tao.

Strengthening the bond with the character and soul comes through the universe. Taoists cultivate practices that involve stillness meditation, ritual, martial arts, qigong, and nourishing life through diet to build connection. One will experience flow by living in harmony with the seasons while accepting what happens. Individuals must know they should only attach their character to the material world to flow through life while experiencing the Tao.

MORAL PRINCIPLES

We routinely fail to maintain moral behavior because of our character's imperfections. Thinking that advances material needs wisdom to serve as a grounding back to cohesiveness and community. As the passing of knowledge continues, philosophy helps direct appropriate sustainability to form the soul in an eternal now. We know we're not formed through answers if the search is everlasting. Therefore, questions promote maturation.

With material time, we can pour our currency of experience into the curiosity of what we perceive to be a reality in real time. By carving into the consciousness of humanity, we tether the soul.

This helps us avoid material suffering and a misplaced position in the cosmos. From the roots of our ancestors, principles that remained true throughout time are recreated through new interpretations of our essence. This is how history repeats itself, allowing each generation its own responsibility for the evolution of being.

CHAPTER 7

NATURAL WORLD

"The future will belong to nature-smart–those individuals, families, businesses, and political leaders who develop a deeper understanding of the transformative power of the natural world and who balance the virtual with the real. The more high-tech we become, the more nature we need."

—Richard Louv

A phenomenon first described in 2005 by journalist Richard Louv is termed "nature-deficit disorder." Louv states this is defined as "human costs of alienating from nature." According to research, it is noted that Americans spend nearly 90 percent of their time indoors, leading to a Western problem in which our species has become disconnected from the natural world. Studies have shown the more we spend time indoors and disconnected from nature, the more significant the increase in depression, anxiety, sleep disorders, and attention problems. As the modern era increased technology, at a cost, we disconnected with our soul.

Consider the survival of our ancestors as they grew knowledge in discovering edible plants and which animals were predators or prey. Learning to travel and build shelter are necessities the modern character will never have to consider as survival. If the sapiens were without the influence of gods, we would be without words to describe their education process. An intuition sparked by nature, our souls pursue the divine of the natural world.

Our species roamed the earth for millions of years, surviving within the natural world. Somehow, we developed a wisdom beyond the resources of forests, rivers, and soil that provided us with the food we eat and the air we breathe. We grew to rely heavily on nature for our health. For instance, the view of a sunrise sets our body clock. The smell of trees and plants fuels our lungs with energy, and the breeze within an open field communicates to our nervous system that we are safe. In every way, the health of our being seeks nature.

Mother Nature's blessings are quite godlike and structured, meaning nature shares duality with our character and exists in a state of being. Beyond the material, we experience a natural flow, which is a familiar feeling for the soul in the presence of God. Within the natural world, we feel connected in a way we can't describe.

Much like God, the energy from nature is abundant. Yet, we treat nature materially, often falling to our humanistic instincts. Clinging to materialism, our egotistical minds shrivel us into believing we are the center of all things. We believe our needs, desires, and resources are what's essential, and we falsely convince ourselves we're capable of controlling the natural world. In relation to the Tao, this would be the law of reverted effect. When we desire immensely to administer our material life, we lose control of it. In a similar fashion, we can't control God in every way, as we can't control nature. Material punishment comes in the form of natural disasters.

Today, modern science seeks to explain the transitional periods of climate and warns us of the dangers we tempt with our destruction of nature, which is not much different from the curriculums of religion or principles of philosophy. Therefore, it's consistent that our ancestors originally worshipped the sun and the moon. Without science, organized religion, or philosophy to back their thinking, a position of vulnerability made it rational to consider nature as God. Even today, we are powerless in the laws of the universe; therefore, the natural world is outside our control.

When we establish a structured hierarchy, religion, or philosophy, the mission is to sustain cooperation. Spiritually, we share this wisdom because survival trumps greed in evolution. Throughout history, however, we have failed regularly and fallen victim to our delusion of need. Exploiting material resources, we take more than required. Overfishing oceans, clearing forests, and polluting rivers have disrupted the natural rhythms of the world. Blindly corrupting the flow of the universe, we dismissed our connection to the source.

INDUSTRIAL REVOLUTION

Think of that spring weather when you open the windows, turn up the music, and feel alive. The breath of fresh air and the restorative power of the sun. There is a sense of mindfulness as we feel loved and cared for. These feelings are mimicked when we delve into our faith, a connection we receive through prayer and meditation. Nature wraps its arms around us to keep us safe and fair-minded, like our belief systems.

For centuries, we have felt these feelings naturally through our environment. At the turn of the eighteenth century, our species transitioned from creating goods by hand to using machines—a point when agricultural societies became industrialized and urban. Beginning in Europe and making its way to America, factories became the means of production.

In an age that created economic growth and new opportunities, people started moving from the countryside into the fast-growing cities. Progress, however, came with a cost, and we experienced significant downsides. With damage to the environment, the health and safety of community hazards negatively impacted our living conditions and disconnected us from the healing powers of nature.

Roman civilization illustrated a kindred experience. When disease and devastating fevers spread through the contamination of food and water, we learned how hazards could wipe through densely packed cities. Rome connected society by land and sea, unlike any empire, and the populated areas experienced slow killers such as tuberculosis and leprosy as a result. The accident of convenience was in our misguided relationship with natural systems, thinking we were above nature as we sought freedom in materialism.

Modern civilization began experiencing similar issues when the Americas were being explored. Technology was rising, and the Industrial Age was a time when society transitioned from an agrarian economy to an economy dominated by industries and machines. As it seemed optimistic, food production increased, which was much needed with the increase in population. The economy improved with the growth of cities and towns, and middle-class citizens were able to catch up financially as wealth became more accessible.

Agriculture had been the largest source of employment until this era. People worked in the fields, producing crops to feed themselves and their communities. For centuries, our characters performed jobs that unconsciously placed us in nature. We were undoubtedly spending time outdoors until the era of speed and comfort moved humanity inside. Machines made it possible to increase the capacity of products like wool and cotton and ended the need for human labor. As our species made the transition to life indoors, we quickly detached our characters from the natural world. Here are a few examples of such changes.

SOCIETAL CHANGES

- People were forced to move to cities to find work in factories.
- Mass production of goods was produced, and life became about material.
- Women joined the workforce.
- Rapid urbanization resulted in crowded cities and poor sanitation—resulting in the spread of disease.

ENVIRONMENTAL CHANGES

- Machines and cities pollute the environment due to chemicals being released by factories.
- Cities became full of trash, and living conditions became poor.
- Air pollution increased.
- Waterways became polluted with oil and debris.
- Carbon dioxide started to be released into Earth's atmosphere.

These were new problems for our species and scenarios we had yet encountered. The impact was not easily noticed and clearly not an issue in the beginning. We overlooked the pollution impact on our planet until decades after the second Industrial Revolution, which occurred at the end of the nineteenth century. For example, scientists didn't realize the depletion of the ozone layer, which is Earth's natural protection against harmful ultraviolet light, until the 1980s.

Under our awareness, air pollution caused a thick blanket of smog from the factories that covered cities, and we began to experience respiratory illness. With excess garbage, we weren't prepared for the proper disposal of sewage, debris, and oil. Our waterways were impacted, reducing the quality of water we drank. Wildlife started to die off as the harmful pollutants drained into rivers, lakes, and oceans.

With technological advancements, we started to drain natural resources, mainly coal, which we needed to heat homes, make iron, and power the factories producing our goods. In the nineteenth century, the coal mining industry boomed, and the use of wood was no longer a priority. Coal, however, would soon be exploited, and we dove into oil and natural gas in the early twentieth century.

The Western world was booming with freedom and entrepreneurship. Wide-eyed and ambitious, the newly independent nation, the United States of America, and the early settlers were after territorial expansion. America increased its population in 1800 from around five million to nearly eighty million people by 1900. Human activity increased as the land and habitats decreased. Hunting and travel soured as we became unstoppable with New Age technology and weapons—an era in which we unconsciously reproduced and overconsumed without knowing the impact on the natural world.

Nearing the end of the twentieth century, the veil was lifted, and we noticed a change. In 1967, the first endangered species list was released, which comprised more than seventy species, and exploitation of land was indirectly affecting the animals. To save our world and resources, the twentieth and twenty-first centuries sparked the rise of laws regarding the environment. Currently, the EPA regularly monitors various environmental health risks and studies how we can better live in harmony with nature.

With altered minds and bodies due to the mass production of food and an indoor lifestyle, our senses became overstimulated. Infectious diseases can now impact the globe in a matter of days, and the necessities we need to survive have become chemically produced, making the task of connecting back to nature seem impossible.

WORLDVIEWS

Worldviews have been constructed regarding nature, like our beliefs in structure around power, religion, and philosophy, which have shaped narration. Attaching the soul to nature helps first to understand the characters we play surrounding it. In pursuit of deepening our connection with the natural world, it is not our job to save it; rather, it is our job to learn from it. To learn from the world's natural resources, we must understand how we interpret them.

We carry three environmental worldviews that shape our beliefs: anthropocentrism, biocentric, and ecocentric. The worldview of anthropocentrism is human-centered, a planetary management worldview that regards humans as separate from and superior to nature, other species, and living organisms such as animals, plants, and mineral resources. These are viewed simply as resources that are available to be exploited for the benefit of all humans justifiably.

The second worldview is biocentric, a stewardship worldview and a perspective of many Native American traditions emphasizing nature and its sacredness. Bio (life) and centric (center), an ethical belief that all living things are valuable. Biocentrism is the perspective that all living things deserve equal moral consideration. Those who support this worldview are focused on animal rights, biodiversity, and the protection of our environment.

The third worldview is ecocentric. According to environmental wisdom, humans and all life forms are interconnected and work as one. This is a perspective that it is in our own self-interest not to harm the overall system. With such an interpretation, it is not Earth that needs managing, as much as we need saving from ourselves.

ANTHROPOCENTRISM

Anthropocentrism literally means human-centered. Philosophically, it is the belief that humans alone possess intrinsic value, meaning that an individual contains the recognition that other beings hold value but only in their ability to serve humans. To many environmentalists, the argument is that anthropocentrism is ethically wrong and is the root of ecological crisis.

Comparable to small- and large-scale human greed, blind actions through anthropocentrism have pushed climate change, ozone depletion, and poisoned water and air. With destruction to the rainforest, abundance of wildfires, decline in biodiversity, and other environmental crises, worldwide species have started becoming extinct.

Glaring concerns pop into the curious mind when considering anthropocentrism among our characters. It is easy to question our egotistical mind as the cause of our planet's demise; however, some evidence suggests it isn't all that bad. Here are the basic principles around the belief.

ANTHROPOCENTRISM BASICS

1. Humans are the most significant beings on Earth, and all other plants, animals, and objects are important only insofar as they support human survival or give humans pleasure.
2. Humans are the central element of the universe.
3. Humans are the final aim of the universe.
4. Humans view and interpret everything in terms of human experience.
5. All life forms that are not human are the only resources to be consumed by human beings.
6. It can be referred to as a point of view that humans are the primary holders of moral standards.

Many forms of misinformation can lead people to believe these philosophies and morals are wrong. Regardless of their accuracy, they are a perspective in our worldview and something we need to recognize and try to understand. For instance, humans must practice self-love to serve those around them, including all living organisms.

We are all selfish to the extent that we need to eat, drink, reproduce, and stay warm. For instance, there is a reason the flight attendant tells the passengers to put their masks on first before assisting others. It is only natural that we seek survival first, care for ourselves first, and then support the world. If our basic needs are met, we are capable of being the solution. As rulers of the animal kingdom, it benefits all if we are first healthy.

Another viewpoint shared is our "life-support system" for humans. Anthropocentrism can be used as motivation for environmental protection and a way to problem-solve how to use the resources within the world to enhance continuation. Collectively, through the lens of survival, we could appropriately structure how we use surrounding resources for sustainability.

First, we must pause and consider that human interests are not all the same, making it rather difficult to distinguish between legitimate and illegitimate intentions across humanity. Therefore, we need to explore the questions of agency, share responsibilities, and fairly attribute blame for predictions regarding the environment.

Measures taken to protect interests and quality of life benefit our environment, and an approach such as anthropocentrism could produce ethically sound communication strategies that work to the world's advantage. The issue arises when we lean on our material understanding and the belief that we had control in the first place. Mother Earth regenerates herself, making us a pawn in the grand scheme. We are no different from the extinct dinosaurs or the variety of species before us that could not adjust to the changing of the planet. As a human race, our ability to question and listen to what the natural world must teach rather than provide answers is a state in which we employ intention from the soul.

Ideally, our eight-billion-person tribe would cooperate rather quickly, as scientists predict a global crisis soon. It is a time in history when the world will have to come together to solve the same problem. Communication among a unified humanity facing the same threat could make us peaceful but also equal. Therefore, an intergenerational approach should shift the curve in evolution, enhancing the consciousness of humanity.

This alone makes the legitimacy of anthropocentrism arguable. However, it is doubtful the globe will ever share the same worldview and values as eco-friendly environments. Therefore, we run into conflict among our beliefs in nature, like the historical wars fighting over religion and power. It becomes a familiar cycle of material suffering through corruption, disagreement, and conflicting beliefs.

BIOCENTRIC AND ECOCENTRIC

Biocentrism is a philosophy that is often the practice of environmentalists. It emphasizes the importance of all living things: animals, plants, and organisms. Biocentrism, compared to ecocentrism, does not place as much value on nonliving components of the environment. However, they are bunched together because they both focus on the protection of nature. Ecocentric differs in that it goes beyond animals, plants, and organisms and places intrinsic value on all nonliving, which are considered rocks, soil, water, and air.

Both philosophies are similar since they recognize the importance of living things, including their environment, while seeking to de-emphasize human importance and promote the value of all creation on the planet. Today, here are examples in which we practice.

BIOCENTRIC EXAMPLE

- Policies around the limitation of hunting to protect grizzly bears.

ECOCENTRIC EXAMPLE

- Policies to protect Alaskan wilderness, which would also protect grizzly bears.

Biocentrism is an ethical approach that practices the perspective of equality. It is a subset of ecocentrism and requires humans to think about their relationship with nature—a philosophy that suggests humans are not superior to other living things and that nature does not exist to be consumed by humans. The concept believes all living things deserve equal moral consideration. Oftentimes, this means fighting for the preservation of biodiversity, animal rights, and protecting the environment.

A philosophy with deep reverence for nature, these principles adhere to the original practice of animism and are recognized among religions today. The first of the five principles of Buddhist ethics states that humans should avoid killing or harming living things. In the Christian religion, Saint Francis of Assisi preached to animals, proclaimed a biocentric theology, and explicitly included animals and plants. Native Americans, who are primarily considered to live harmoniously with nature, find all living beings and natural objects to have some sacred value.

Ecocentrism is broad and recognizes Earth as the ultimate source of value, which makes it directly opposed to anthropocentrism. The philosophy is that Earth is the center of all ethical, intellectual, and practical deliberations, a belief that Earth needs everything within it to sustain its well-being, and in the power of Earth's existence, we find meaning and enablement for all beings.

Oftentimes, ecocentrics will urge humans to be self-limited to remain sustainable because the idea is that human selfishness destroys ecological integrity. For example, surface mining, including strip mining, harms the environment but can make natural resources available for human populations. Ecocentrism fights against these tactics solely because it harms the environment. Therefore, mining is wrong because the perspective of all natural things having inherent moral values makes exploitation immoral.

CONNECTION WITH THE NATURAL WORLD

Consciousness grows in the form of awareness. Psychologically, our aim is to build the muscle of mindfulness while living in a state of flow with our soul. Aligning the character with natural forces aids spiritual suffering. This is one of the many reasons people feel incredibly connected when they hike or seek retreat in the woods. The universe starts to unravel itself to the character, and unexplained emotions creep into their awareness.

Ralph Waldo Emerson, a philosopher who led the transcendentalist movement in the nineteenth century, writes in *Nature* that nature is the body of God's soul: "Every moment instructs, and every object; for wisdom is infused into every form. It has been poured into us as blood; it convulsed us as pain; it slid into us as pleasure; it enveloped us in dull, melancholy days, or in days of cheerful labor; we did not guess its essence until after a long time."

Consider the human organism itself as nature, which helps us consider the influence of natural settings. Our early philosophers emphasized that humans are habitual and that much of our behavior is related to the environment around us. This happens because, naturally, we fall unconscious to the environment and become a byproduct of our surroundings. As Aristotle put it, "We are what we repeatedly do." In the sense that we connect with nature, we are what we repeatedly do.

If we are disconnected from the natural world, we habitually become something else. The modern era, specifically the twentieth century until now, is the reality of disconnection from nature. Our shift out of natural settings and nature-connected communities is the byproduct of twenty-first-century species. This does not mean the doom of humanity or the end of our evolution; it is more so a reflective process of where we go from here.

Our ancestors were connected to the natural world, as were the agrarian cultures. Proving our capabilities, we are beginning to recognize the importance of our surroundings, and it is one of the main reasons why major corporations are going green. They understand the positive impact green spaces provide for people and their habits. Natural sunlight, green spaces, and fresh air within the office allow workers and customers to think clearly. It optimizes human behavior and enhances our overall mood and well-being solely because of the environment.

The issue we're now facing among humanity is financial. Economies are run by machines, and civilization is indoors. A gap in financial power may not be a new problem; however, our working conditions are. Not only have we furthered the separation of power through money—but now the environment. If you can't afford to create or build an environment to support you and your community, you are unlikely to thrive. Our overconsumption and population growth have deepened the human environmental impact and, consequently, the impoverishment of living. We know environments shape consciousness, and to be healthy in the modern era, it pays to be wealthy.

Since human competency lost touch with the ability to live in harmony with the land, people can no longer fuel themselves from their property. We've become dependent on a system outside ourselves for support, in which society generates through machinery. Therefore, the quality of living directly reflects one's relationship with wealth, meaning the wealthier you are, the healthier you are. This creates a massive divide among our people and causes modern diseases. For example, mental health issues rise in overstimulated cities, respiratory issues increase from poor air quality, and obesity comes from overconsumption of processed foods.

We've learned that environments change and living organisms evolve with them. We are no different today, except for most of history; we have done the process naturally. The last few centuries have seemed different as we have become the planet's dominant species. The trajectory has been on that path for centuries, but the boom of industrialization fully solidified our position of power. In many regards, we not only rule the top of the food chain among animals and plants, but we're the controllers of nature.

We now change and often degrade Earth's environments, a global issue that should incentivize us to create systems of natural settings in urbanized cities by restructuring society to work in harmony with nature.

WE ARE NATURE

When we connect with the natural world, we become mindful of the species within it. Being conscious, we can understand what is happening inside us and the connection we share with all living organisms. For example, the animals and species live and die in accordance with the law of the land, and in perfect harmony, they are interconnected with the cosmos. They may not have developed the brain capacity that humans have and are not fully capable of developing technologies for comfort. However, we are not far off biologically from these organisms. We, too, live in accordance with the land.

It may not be the most leisurely lifestyle to dissociate ourselves from modern technology and indoor comfort, but beneath our skin runs a network of veins, arteries, and capillaries that, if carried out, could stretch around Earth 2.5 times. The complexity that lives inside us needs the diversity that nature supplies. The body's natural hardwiring needs the sun's fuel and Earth's oxygen to keep us alive. Our bodies use the modalities to keep our inner complexities in balance. Environmental stress harms not only plants and animals but humans as well. When our air gets polluted, we get polluted. When exposed to urbanized pollutants like sound and artificial light, we, too, start to become dysfunctional.

Like the roots of a tree, a tree begins with a sprout and starts a developmental process. Immature blood vessels and cells will mature and grow to eventually become a network of connections that allow trees to live. As a seed, the maturation process grows into a fully functional tree with awareness.

For instance, trees in nature share water and nutrients through networks to communicate and aid other trees' health. They go as far as sending distress signals about drought and disease. An example would be an insect attacking a tree. Different trees will begin to alter their behavior once they receive the messages. Through what's called mycorrhizal networks, they send chemical and electrical signals through the vast web of wood. The tree must be aware of its surroundings, maintain health, and support the community around them. We share these same traits with the trees through awareness. They possess a developed root brain, which works as their conscious mind. It will analyze incoming data and generate responses to solve problems.

It may be language that makes humans unique, but complexity requires awareness. Consciousness is equated, making awareness shared among all living organisms because it requires assessment—an assessment that makes all organisms aware of their surroundings. Organisms will modify their behavior to improve the chances of survival.

Plants operate a molecular and electrical system, whereas animals are more neural. Sharing awareness, all living species become interconnected through a source. Displaying a character and soul, the source produces a frequency at which energy vibrates. What this source is cannot be defined. Therefore, we turn back around to the possibility of nature being divine.

Our connection to this vibration comes through a sensory experience. When we are present, frequently in nature, we begin to feel its power. Everything in our being starts to change, and without words, we seek into our own nature. By consciously removing ourselves from the indoor lifestyle, we receive the diversity needed to maintain awareness.

CHAPTER 8

SENSORY EXPERIENCE

Our characters experience the world around us through the feedback loops of our senses. When seeking to understand human nature, the most outstanding teacher is nature. From cold to hot, wet to dry, and light to dark, we are the entire ecosystem in and of itself. Materially, we live out patterns based on the recognition of what we know—patterns related to our level of awareness and the quality of our health. When we are disconnected from our senses, we are disconnected from the source. Without knowing who we are, we can't trust the feedback we receive from our environment. This misunderstanding is a dysfunction within our senses and directs us toward material suffering.

Energy flows around the planet to the molecules living inside us. From the microbes that originated from creation to the chemistry in our bodies today, we are a part of nature. Our immune system is a sensory system that constantly communicates throughout the body—from our endocrine and nervous systems to our environment. Our mind and body are connected to the outer world, giving feedback loops autonomously and without permission. When we explore the archaic brain functioning as our reptilian self, we begin the process of narrowing into the roots of our evolutionary history. We become neurobiologically connected as we get exposed to the gifts of Mother Nature and ignited by vibrations within the environment. This is the state of wholeness between being and existing without words.

The frequencies we receive from the natural world impact how we feel within our states of being. Our level of awareness dictates the level of consciousness we experience. For example, breathing is a foundational teaching across religions and philosophies because respiration maintains metabolic functions. Breathing sustains life force and directly reflects what is happening in the environment. It is the only unconscious system receiving feedback from stimuli around us that we can control. This makes it a tool from the source of nature to build awareness.

Energy is everywhere, and all living organisms are the same. Breathing coexists with the vibrations of the planet, connecting us as one. For instance, photosynthesis, which ignites the atmosphere, empowers our plants. The life cycle thrives around plants in nontoxic areas because plants can breathe. When environments are toxic, with high pollution, both humans and living organisms experience dysfunctional breathing. When in poisonous energy fields, our senses become overly aroused and fall out of balance.

Being out of balance drastically disrupts our organism's natural rhythm and life force. The frequencies get clogged inside our body, and we experience chronic stress. As dysfunction resides in the energy field, our character feels anxious and depressed. Therefore, it is valuable for us to learn the stimuli occurring around our senses. When we can increase self-knowledge of who we are, we can expand and trust the wisdom of our souls.

NATURE HEALS

When we encounter nature, we reduce stress. Mental fatigue is reduced, blood flow is promoted, and our mood is bolstered. As a species, we were developed in nature and learned to work with its natural forces throughout evolution. With closer connection, our awareness was likely to have been more significant, and our intuition was much higher. Before writing or complex communication, consider the wisdom of our ancestors. For much of life, we were without a written blueprint for survival. Our unique ability to express our soul evolved the expressions of our character, and we found ways to adapt to our world intuitively.

Today's world finds progress in the process of unlearning the character to gain an understanding of the soul. As the pendulum of awareness continues to shift toward artificial existence, the process of mindful practice guides the character toward spiritual suffering, and we can be without words. This is the power of simply being in the natural world. We come to know its complexity by merely connecting with it. Mindful wandering brings us closer to the source and strengthens sensory awareness.

To better understand our character's health, we must consider the human organism as a battery charged by unplugging from the material world and receiving its power within nature. Here are the senses of awareness we use to navigate the natural world.

SENSATIONAL AWARENESS: FIVE SENSES

1. Sight (vision)—a famous study about nature is found in an experiment that compared patients who had a view of trees versus those who viewed a brick wall. The patients with a view of trees went home sooner, felt better emotionally, and

had fewer negative notes from nurses.
2. Sound (hearing)—a study found that bird sounds allow people to recover from stress faster. A study in America showed that 91 percent of people said they visit natural parks to enjoy the natural sounds, such as running water.
3. Smell (breathing)—traditionally, aromatherapy affects mood and relaxation. For example, beeswax has been found to make people happier, and spiced apples and lavender alter people's brainwaves.
4. Touch (skin)—our skin is the body's largest organ. Therefore, we feel connected when we connect with nature and living organisms. For example, touching animals has routinely been shown to improve the quality of our hearts. Petting a dog is less stressful than talking to a person, which is why dogs are used in companion therapy to aid in lowering heart rate and relaxing psychiatric patients. Another form of health from touch is "grounding," which connects our bare skin to the earth. Grounding has been shown to improve our body's physiology and the immune system simply by placing our bare feet in the ground's natural sources.
5. Taste—a unique sense, it provides information about the food we're eating. An example can be the comparison of sweet and bitter. When we taste something sweet, like a fresh apple, we tend to enjoy it. When we taste something bitter, we spit it out. Bitter flavors are indicative of toxins in foods, and our body warns us not to eat them. This is why healthier and natural foods are asso-

ciated with less anxiety and depression.

CHRONIC STRESS

Much of how we respond to moments in life is prompted by the senses of the mind and body, which are based on the environment around us. Often, we feel irritable or emotional and trap ourselves inside our character without ever considering the external environment. This low level of awareness disconnects us from our inner wisdom.

Modern life is busy, and its chaos often manipulates our being into an unhealthy awareness. Natural breathing, for example. If we are stuck indoors and inhaling toxic air, our breathing signals a response to the mind and body. Beneath our conscious mind, our breathing will slowly pick up toxic particles through the nose. The nose hairs and sinuses get clogged, dropping the jaw, and we breathe through our mouths. Since no defense mechanisms inside the mouth block toxic air from entering our lungs, we will overwork our body's immune system and become sick.

Any instances of unconscious mouth breathing disrupt our quality of life. Since the nose is meant for breathing, it should be the only means of oxygen intake outside of hard labor or nearby threats. Before language, our ancestors intuitively knew we needed to run if the mouth was open. Today, we should only need to breathe through our mouths in moments of intense exercise or when we eat food or talk with others. With corruption to natural environments, our artificial existence has disrupted the frequencies our unconscious receives and frequently leaves the vibrational field of our body dysfunctional. In many cases, this has created the modern disease of mental illness by simply keeping our material existence in chronic stress.

Since the Industrial Age, modern society has become chronic mouth breathers, which indicates our disconnect from nature.

George Catlin is widely credited for such a discovery. In the nineteenth century, he wrote a book titled *Shut Your Mouth and Save Your Life*. He painted the faces of indigenous people among the North American Plains and noticed the superior health of the tribes he visited. Over time, he concluded that their vigorous practice was breathing through the nose.

Mothers breastfed much longer than the settlers, strengthening their children's jaws. The parents would also routinely close the lips of their children's mouths to promote nasal breathing, especially during sleep. Native Americans knew sleeping with an open mouth was far from natural. Catlin suggested that no other animals apart from humans slept with their mouths open. He also concluded that these tribes understood that habits against nature would lead to symptoms and disease.

By way of his illustrations, children could often be found sleeping outside where the air was fresh and cold. This showed the tribe's wisdom in knowing when children were hot; they would breathe through their mouths to expel heat. The indigenous tribes, living in accordance with the land, knew and understood that nature designed us to breathe correctly, and it's worth noting that these tribes were removed from industrial impact.

Incomparably, tribes from North to South America were significantly connected to the natural world before the takeover of the American nation during the nineteenth century. They were without technological advances that mass-produced food and were not impacted by poor air quality and noise pollution. To our knowledge, Native Americans were still practicing agrarian culture and animistic religions, which maintained a connection to the natural world and an intuitive sense of human health.

During the industrial period, those losing connection to nature noticed the jaw structure and anatomy of the body change. This caused a population of people to become chronic mouth breathers, leading to New Age issues such as sleep apnea. An age of increased smoking and air pollution added a layer of concern, creating chronic obstructive pulmonary disease (COPD), which is now the third leading cause of death worldwide.

A primarily held theory is that we became mouth breathers from the lack of chewing food, a consequence of mass food production. To feed large numbers of people, our food became processed and softer. We were not only eating food of less quality but using our jaws less to chew. There was less of a need to be breastfed compared to indigenous mothers. As a result, the jaw structure weakened in children, and anatomy degenerated over the centuries.

This became an issue because mouth breathing is a natural response built within the human organism to respond to threats. When we breathe through our mouth, we mechanically breathe into our upper chest, which has been used evolutionarily to process oxygen in the upper lungs to activate our sympathetic nervous system. The sympathetic system is our fight-or-flight response to the environment and is used in times of threat.

By becoming chronic mouth breathers, our nervous system believes itself to be in a constant state of stress. Underneath our awareness, the body's alarm system, which nature created to operate acutely, is being exercised on a regular basis. Continuous use tricks the system into thinking there is always a lion nearby. If we're in a chronic state of anxiety, we don't have the space available to be whole.

Breathing is not our only concern. Another is exposure to noise pollution. An overloaded auditory stress is not only associated with general annoyance but also disrupts sleep patterns. This adversely affects the cardiovascular system, creating chronic stress on our entire organism. Specifically, the heart—heart disease is now the leading cause of death in the US.

Noise from road traffic, streetlights, generators, and planes exposes us to metabolic dysfunctions. A study out of Europe and the European Environment Agency (EEA) even found noise contributes to 48,000 new cases of ischemic heart disease a year and 12,000 premature deaths. With the overload of these sensory stimulations, the dysfunctional awareness of our character disconnects our soul from the natural world. Not only do we lose a sense of who we are, but our character's health is diminished.

LIFE FORCE

Many beliefs surround the idea that our heritage causes modern health issues. Therefore, we're confident that we have control over our health by taking pharmaceutical drugs. If it's high blood pressure that plagues the family tree, medicine can fix it. Often, this is the argument and ammo required to blame the genes of our heritage. In a material world, operating on speed and money creates an easy sell for big corporations wanting to sell medication to alleviate suffering.

An individual who considers themselves not to have time or the desire to be responsible for their own health completely disregards the natural life forces within nature. Therefore, the only option is habitually living unconsciously within the system around you—a system of industry materialism, no longer the source of nature.

In our opportunity to learn about the self, we often delegate health to the material. However, awareness can open consciousness and allow us to hear the narration told by the spirit of nature. When we tether the natural world, the more prevalent our intuition becomes. In time, we become aware of the loops in our energy field and radiate sustained mindfulness.

Considering the importance of breathing, we can study other living organisms life force. A representative case is when plants breathe in carbon dioxide and release oxygen; when we breathe in oxygen, we release carbon dioxide. Our anatomy resembles these plant processes inside the airways and down to the lungs. For instance, the passageways of our lungs are shaped like broccoli, where our bronchi and bronchioles live. Our tiny sac alveoli are shaped like grapes sitting inside our lungs. Blood vessels and circulation flowing throughout the body provide a road map painted like the core of a beet. Ironically, these foods serve positive benefits for the health of our body, and their symbolism is nature's way of teaching us.

Eating natural produce, such as broccoli and grapes, opens our airways and fights free radicals through the increase of antioxidant enzymes, helping us breathe. When we breathe in polluted air, pollen, or other forms of poor-quality air, grapes provide powerful antioxidants and anti-inflammatories and have even been shown to suppress lung inflammation caused by COPD.

Our grape-like alveoli sacs open and close with the transfer of breaths, just like a fine wine. Beetroot, another example, is rich in nitrates, which benefit lung function. Nitrates relax blood vessels, reduce blood pressure, and optimize the amount of oxygen we intake. This explains elite athletes' use of beet supplementation because beetroot production creates two significant physiological effects: widening blood vessels and lowering blood pressure to improve blood flow.

Furthermore, the nervous system is fueled by the electricity of Earth's surface, and our arteries and veins overlap like the roots of a tree. Like a tree, our arteries carry oxygenated blood from the heart to the body's tissues. Veins then carry oxygen-depleted blood from the tissues to the heart. Capillaries and tiny blood vessels connect arteries to veins, completing the process.

This process keeps us alive and feeds the appropriate nutrients needed to maintain life force. It is also the exact process that exists within the roots of a tree through its core, into the branches and leaves. Trees play a vital role in the ecosystem by keeping us alive and speaking to us in a way that makes us feel safe. Trees even deepen our awareness by providing rootedness and shelter, making us feel connected to something larger than ourselves.

Calling us closer to mindfulness, trees are similar within consciousness in that they store memories and communicate with each other. Standing upright, with a central trunk and mobile limbs, the pattern of branches represent the bronchi in our lungs as they, too, breathe. Like plant life, trees release oxygen for our survival, and when we align with these natural forces, we become aware of natures medicine.

BIOPHILIA

The harmony in nature's green spaces releases vibrations that impact our minds and bodies. We can speed up the process of downshifting out of aroused environments and get back to the refueling process by reconnecting with nature. Adaptation tones in natural settings help us regain energy when we voluntarily spend time in green environments. Respiration slows down, and blood pressure decreases, which eases the system of our character. Our primal, unconscious brain feels safe and reduces stress levels by enhancing concentration, and we become mindful. Naturally, we develop a space that connects us without words.

The most effective way to downshift a nervous system is to spend time with the source in quiet, natural spaces. This soothes the nervous system and naturally builds meditative states. This is called the biophilia effect, the sensory experience felt through nature: sight, sound, smell, touch, and taste. Feedback loops to our awareness are based upon the recognition of these sensory experiences.

Through vibration, the source communicates from the natural world to our being through the senses. For example, the breath triggers the brain in response to external stimuli coming through the environment. When we feel frightened, our response is to open our mouths to get more air, forcing us to use the upper chest and shoulders to breathe. This will exhaust our auxiliary muscles and lessen our exchange of oxygen in the body. This type of breathing triggers our brainstem and puts our mind on alert, predicting the severity of the threat. We can downshift in such instances with our breathing, reconnect with nature, and align our nervous system with green spaces. This will invite space for the soul, and the source of nature will guide awareness.

HEALING POWERS

There are various ways to connect with our soul by implementing tangible tools existing in nature, and it is essential to develop structure around these perspectives. As the modern human continues to expand in the technological realm of today's existence, we should now more than ever consider our relationship with the natural world objectively. In a way, we need to deliberately seek discomfort while rewilding ourselves back to our ancestral roots.

Nature has positive effects on our mood and cognitive function, including working memory and dampening the impact on anxiety, creating space for wholeness and the source to build awareness. First, we must slowly consider and process the elements of the human body. One must acknowledge the working systems of both our stress and adaptive processes. The character's body is heavily controlled by a nervous system, which includes two subsystems. The central nervous system provides for our brain and spinal cord, and the peripheral nervous system provides for the part of our nervous system that isn't our brain and spinal cord. Within the peripheral nervous system, there is another set of subsystems: the somatic nervous system and the autonomic nervous system.

The somatic nervous system includes the muscles we can control, plus all the nerves throughout the body that carry information from our senses. Our autonomic nervous system is the part of our nervous system that connects our brain to almost all our internal organs. Nature primarily impacts the stimulation of our muscles, senses, and unconscious processes in the mind and body. As we become mindful of these processes, we tend to sort out the appropriate timing and dosage we individually need in nature. By acknowledging the basic foundations of our body's processes, we can activate the soul.

NATURE'S TOOLKIT

By activating the senses, our body's nervous system will begin to wire itself and build intuition. We gain awareness of the energy fields around us with the vibration of the source. These practices have been used for centuries and can now serve in our rewilding path. From a holistic perspective and ancient philosophy, nature awakens our chakras—a Sanskrit word that means "wheel" or "disk" as it refers to the body's energy centers.

Each chakra is spinning energy connected to specific nerve bundles and major organs. It regulates the body's processes, such as organ functioning, immunity, and emotions. Chakras are present along the spinal cord and activated through different vibrational frequencies and functions.

We have seven chakras aligned within the body. The upper three are our mental and spiritual chakras, the lower three are our physical chakras, and the heart chakra in the middle bridges the upper and lower chakras, creating balance.

The chakras are a philosophy we've come to accept and recognize through cultures of Hinduism and Buddhism. Beginning at the base and ascending to the crown of the head, each chakra is associated with a particular sound, color, and aspect of consciousness. They are all responsible for governing our physical, emotional, and spiritual functions.

Many tangible practices can be used to release, empower, and activate the chakras. Whether through breathwork, sound baths, grounding, or deliberate stressors, the objective of health is being physically, mentally, and spiritually aligned with the energy forces around you. When the mind and body are fully functioning, we create a space for our energetic field to connect without words. Here is an overview of the chakra system within the body.

THE SEVEN CHAKRAS

1. Root (Muladhara)—associated with survival, stability, and grounding and located at the base of the spine. Think safety when considering the root. It is connected to the musical "C" note and the color red.
2. Sacral (Svadhisthana)—associated with creativity, sexuality, and emotional balance and located in the lower abdomen. Think creation when considering the sacral. It is connected to the musical "D" note and the color orange.
3. Solar plexus (Manipura)—associated with personal power, self-confidence, and digestion and located in the upper abdomen. Think ego when considering the solar plexus. It is connected to the musical "E" note and the color yellow.
4. Heart (Anahata)—associated with love, compas-

sion, and emotional well-being and located in the center of the chest. Think of unity when considering the heart. It is connected to the musical "F" note and the color green.
5. Throat (Vishuddha)—associated with communication, self-expression, and authenticity and located in the throat. Think authentic when considering the throat. It is connected to the musical "G" note and the color blue.
6. Third eye (Ajna)—associated with intuition, perception, and spiritual insight and located between the eyebrows. Think about imagination when considering the third eye. It is connected to the musical "A" note and the color indigo.
7. Crown (Sahasrara)—associated with consciousness, enlightenment, and connection to the divine and located at the top of the head. Think of the source when considering the crown. It is connected to the musical "B" note and the color violet.

AURA FIELD

An aura field is described as a subtle body, a concept from ancient Indian philosophy that describes the being other than the physical body. A term from Western philosophy oftentimes considers aura as the psyche. Aura within this section is an electromagnetic field around the living body of our character. Whereas the chakras are a system within the body, running along the spine, our aura is a colored emanation that encloses the body.

Aura surrounds all living things, including animals and plants, and changes energy based on thoughts, feelings, and experiences. The energy field around living species radiates in an oval shape and has seven layers. Each layer is related to the seven energy chakras within the body, where aura is composed of layer upon layer of outer energy and consciousness. Visualize each layer as a body, fully alive and functioning.

In a world of its own, each layer is immersed within the space in which we experience the material world. The physical layer of the aura is composed of three levels: etheric, emotional, and mental. The astral layer is the bridge between the spiritual and physical. The spiritual plane is above the astral layer and holds our gradations of enlightenment. Our spiritual bodies have three layers: the etheric template, the celestial level, and the ketheric template.

When our mind and body align with the soul, we can manifest or create within the material world because of our connection with the electromagnetic field surrounding us. For instance, when a belief is transmitted from the source through our high levels of aura, we can process it down into the denser levels of material until we fully crystallize it into reality. Without words, the gift of our soul comes into this material life for the collective consciousness. As we express ourselves fully, we experience spiritual suffering within material reality. When attending to the needs of our energy fields, both outer and inner, we step into our life's work with clarity and awareness.

Energy is impacted by surrounding environments. Our aura can be quickly zapped around toxic people and places. Identical to plant life, if the surrounding environment is polluted, we disrupt the life force and disconnect from our sensory experience. In the modern era, filled with convenience, our characters are less exposed to the mindful wandering that takes place in natural environments. With overstimulated senses, we deplete our energy field and materially suffer from our illnesses. As we unlearn the current character, being without words, we must associate with the vibrational field of nature to reawaken who we are.

Here is an overview of the aura field surrounding the body.

SEVEN LAYERS OF THE AURA

1. Etheric layer—closest to the body, within one to two inches from the surface of the skin. Connected to our root chakra.
2. Emotional layer—three inches away from the body and connected to our emotions. This layer is connected to our sacral.
3. Mental layer—sitting about three to eight inches away from the body. This layer deals with our thought processes and is connected to the solar plexus.
4. Astral layer—connected to the heart chakra. This layer acts as the bridge between physical and spiritual energy.
5. Etheric template—considered the blueprint and exists on the physical plane. It is connected to the throat chakra.
6. Celestial layer—connected to our third eye. This layer starts our spiritual alignment. It can be considered a space where we experience unconditional love.
7. Ketheric template—the highest spiritual layer connected to the crown chakra. At this level of energy, we are connected to our psychic abilities.

CHAPTER 9

MIND-BODY CONNECTION

Operating existence with our being, our mind and body must be healthy. If the mind-body connection is sustainable, it awards us more time to express our soul. Directing attention toward structure, with basic principles, our health relies on breathing, nutrition, movement, and sleep to thrive. When we move throughout our day with energy, we can accomplish tasks and acquire new experiences.

Holistic health in the modern era is aligning back with nature. When the Industrial Age created artificial environments and the imposition of new work disciplines, we watched the natural rhythms of our bodies get disrupted. Mouth breathing, processed foods, sedentary lifestyles, and overexposure to artificial sound and light have placed our nervous system into chronic stress states, often clogging our chakras and disrupting our relationship with our aura.

Chronic stress places our character in a state of anxiety, and our ambition to spiritually suffer gets diminished as we chase materialism. Today, our awareness of our surroundings fights to be heightened because the everyday environment controlling our senses is filled with pollution. From the sounds we hear to the air we breathe, our unconscious is overwhelmed and harms our perspective. Therefore, one must integrate themselves back into the world's natural rhythms and align their senses with the biological structure of the cosmos.

In the process, you will feel the space provided for the soul to enter experience without words. Use one or all components as a daily practice to live in accordance with nature. Each section will provide a brief outline of the structure to follow. However, each person must learn the timing and dosage of these practices on their own. Through time, the intention of repetitive practice will keep the body's disks clear and the energy field open. This will open consciousness to higher realms and allow the soul to fully experience material existence.

PART I: AWAKEN THE SENSES

SIGHT: SUN GAZING

Our sight and sense of vision are unique because they are technically part of our brain. The retina and optic nerve are structured as a piece of our brain and within the central nervous system. Therefore, it's essential to be aware of it and its power. For instance, our sight needs the sun to set our circadian rhythm. The circadian rhythm is our organism's physical, mental, and behavioral changes that follow a twenty-four-hour cycle. Considered our internal clock, the brain regulates cycles of alertness and sleepiness by responding to light changes in the environment, making it crucial that our eyes are in tune with sunlight.

Sun gazing has become a top priority for modern health because of our lack of sunlight and increased screen usage. We now primarily live underneath artificial light, specifically blue light screens, late into the evening. Misaligning our connection to the natural world, we disrupt our internal processes through travel and work that don't allow for a consistent sleep schedule.

It may be common knowledge that staring directly at the sun is detrimental. However, a meditative practice called sun gazing is the appropriate way to clear the mind. Seeing the sun's rising or setting decreases the sun's intensity, and our vision naturally sees the sky through a wide lens. The intentions are to view the surrounding area of the sun rather than staring directly at it.

The light around sunrise and sunset develops a panoramic view that relaxes our pupils, eliciting a soothing response from our eyes to the brain and throughout the entire body. By implementing sun gazing into our daily routine, we integrate ourselves with nature's soul. It is a natural way to worship the energy of the source.

For instance, melatonin is a hormone secreted by our body. It is essential for sleep. The sun directly impacts this hormonal secretion. Consider how alive and awake your body feels during the summer. The sun is out longer and delays melatonin secretion, making us more active. When we are exposed to morning sunlight, the eyes pick up information from the sun that increases cortisol. This is positive for our mood as it makes us alert and sets a timer to prepare us for bed later in the evening. When the sun sets and darkens, our body produces melatonin, preparing us for sleep. This happens because of the sun's attachment to our circadian rhythm.

It's also why we sleep longer in the winter. Simply being outside assists our body in naturally regulating melatonin. As this process takes place, our stress levels lower, and we notice a decrease in reactivity. As we decrease the fight-or-flight response, space opens to the soul. In part, this explains why specific individuals experience seasonal depression.

Contemplate the character as a battery and the sun as a charger. We must regularly charge our nervous system to armor ourselves with durability. A repetitive input from the sun awakens us to vitality and a deepened sense of purpose. We cleanse the disks along our spine and illuminate the colors of our aura field. Living a life in alignment opens the space needed for the source to work through us.

SOUND BATH

A long-standing holistic practice is within the power of sound and the healing we receive. In fact, many religious beliefs and evolutionary theories believe the world began with sound. Whether the big bang or the "Word" of the Lord, sound penetrates the soul of humanity. In Hindu tradition, the sound of "Om" is believed to contain the entire universe. For instance, the vibration we receive when making the sound "AUM" causes our body to experience 432 hertz (Hz), the same vibration of anything and everything found in nature. Said to exist without time, creating such sound starts at the back of our throats, through our mouths, and into our lips, making three syllables. Additionally, we follow the vibration when our lips are closed in silence. This means the sound is past, present, and future, followed by silence, creating a comprehension we experience without words.

In the material world, Aboriginal didgeridoos are believed to be the oldest musical instruments and have been found in cave paintings that are thousands of years old. When played, it induces the brain states immediately and brings our mind and body to the present. As the sound from the instrument calms our being, we open space for the state of becoming. Tibetan singing bowls are another example of sound bathing traced back thousands of years. We discovered that the metal and alloys from meteorites created sounds and vibrations that eased physiological tension.

Two major regions of the world, China, which used gongs, and the Greeks, who used sound frequencies, explored sound for healing as well. The resonance and vibrations of such instruments were used to treat a variety of health ailments, such as indigestion, insomnia, and mental disturbances. Aristotle, for example, frequently referenced how music helped purify the soul.

Today, sound baths are used to nurture emotional and mental well-being. For example, the vagus nerve is a critical component of the parasympathetic nervous system, the state of relaxation. When we consciously relax and release tension with sound guidance, we activate the vagus nerve. Sound healing is an alternative therapy used to trigger the relaxation of the nerves of the body. In a calm state, we bring awareness to the brain waves within the mind that calm the body and open space for the soul to bring in source energy.

Sound bathing can be performed individually, for others, or in groups. Like jazz, there is no set way to play music using natural instruments. The focus is to play sounds and create vibrations that will penetrate the mind and body. These vibrations often open the chakras and release any blockage lingering throughout the system, while simultaneously cleansing the aura field around our body.

In modern sound bathing, instruments such as crystal bowls, Tibetan bowls, drums, gongs, wind chimes, and rain sticks are standard practices. The instruments harmonize and create a frequency in the spiritual world while participating in the material. During a session, it is not uncommon for individuals to experience emotions or release mental tension. The sound helps shake the nervous system free, which adapts the entire human organism and awakens the soul. As the sensation of stress leaves the character, we experience a space of silence.

SMELL: BREATHING

We understand energy within our soul by the way we breathe. For instance, in Christianity, the Holy Spirit is often considered a breath or wind. A representative case is in the Hebrew Bible; the word "Ruach" refers to God as a breath, a wind, or a life force that sustains all living things. Universally, breath gives life and is the core of our physical nature. Without the breath, we are unable to experience material existence.

Breath is vital because it is the only controllable resource in our physiology. We, therefore, can manage our breathing to influence the autonomic nervous system. The most effective way to bring us back to nature is to connect with our breathing and control physiology. The driver of physiological transformation is parasympathetic, our state of adaptation. This is where we regenerate, recreate, and open space for the soul. This makes the first principle in vitality to maintain slow respiration and recognition. As discussed earlier, the value of breathing through the nose retains a sustainable energy system and keeps us functioning correctly. Quiet and rhythmic nasal breathing is the base of all understanding.

Modern science explains the value of our breath today; however, this knowledge has been around for centuries. Often covered with mindful and meditative practices, the foundational principle throughout history has been building an alliance with one's breath. This has been known and credited because our autonomic nervous system is active and governed by the sympathetic and parasympathetic state. These states directly reflect how we breathe and can disrupt perspective if we allow it to go unconscious.

Even when we're asleep, these nervous systems control both the fight-or-flight and rest-and-digest processes in our body. For instance, the sympathetic nervous system refers to stress and is used for acute responses to fight-or-flight scenarios. The parasympathetic nervous system refers to recovery and relaxes the body after periods of stress or danger. Since breathing happens below our conscious mind, mismanaging can become easy.

For instance, when we're asleep, our jaw can drop while breathing. The tongue falls into the back of the mouth, and a cascade of adverse effects occurs. Typically, we begin to snore, our mouth becomes dry, and oftentimes, we stop breathing. In the case of obstruction, sleep apnea becomes the symptom of snoring. Apnea, meaning "no breath," is a temporary but repeated stopping and starting of breath and is associated with health problems such as heart attack and strokes.

When we deepen our relationship with breathing, we begin to feel the power of the source, and one way to experience this is by learning to connect with our aura. Since aura contains the electromagnetic field that we emit within and just outside our body, it is regarded as essential for life force. In the stillness of our breath, we begin to feel this energy, and the source will then showcase its power and align us with spiritual suffering. Returning to material reality following a breath practice will allow us to experience life and the characters we play fully.

It is best to begin awareness of our breath by spending time throughout the day focusing attention on breathing quietly and softly through the nose. Beyond consistent nasal breathing, it benefits our characters' energy fields to focus on controlled cadence breathing. This means sitting still and following the breath in through the nose for the same amount of time on the inhalation and exhalation. A specific protocol is inhaling through the nose for five seconds with a pause. Following the pause, exhale through the nose for five seconds with a pause. Repeat this cycle until you feel the nervous system begin to quiet.

TOUCH: EARTH'S ENERGY FIELDS

A term known as "earthing" refers to contact with the earth's surface electrons by walking barefoot outside, sleeping, or sitting with conductive systems. This happens because electricity, including our nervous system, needs to be charged within the cosmos. When we integrate spiritual practices into our daily lives, such as grounding to the earth, we meet with a realm that heightens our consciousness. By plugging into Mother Nature, our cells are specialized to conduct electrical currents from the earth. Electricity is required for our nervous system to charge the mind and body, explaining the benefits of grounding our bare feet to the earth's surface.

Grounding our bodies has been shown to improve our health by transferring energy from the earth into our bodies. The earth can control the shifting from sympathetic to parasympathetic states, and when we allow the energy from the ground to adapt to our state, electrical signaling improves movement, thoughts, and feelings.

When the modern lifestyle was separated from Earth's energy during the Industrial Age, the result was higher respiration rates, weak bone density, low endurance, poor stability, and overstimulated minds. By simply connecting with the power of the earth, we begin to heal. To rewild our system back to nature, we must now be consciously aware of finding time to ground our bodies to the earth.

Throughout the world, you can find pockets where the earth's energy is high. From hot springs, salt caves, and energy vortexes, the planet supplies what is needed to heal our systems. For example, Germany has the Berchtesgaden Salt Mine. Salt, one of the most essential minerals in the world, can alleviate allergies and respiratory illness. Sedona, Arizona, has vortices, swirling centers of energy that affect our physical, emotional, and spiritual well-being. New Mexico is the host to the Jemez Hot Springs, where geothermal water sources produce rich minerals such as calcium, lithium, magnesium, potassium, iron, and silica to benefit the mind and body through the skin. A soak in these hot springs allows us to absorb the minerals through our skin to heal our mind and body.

Yellowstone National Park in the United States grabs most of the attention for hot springs and geysers, which are the manifestation of volcanic activity. Still, you can find healing hot springs throughout the world. In Central America, the Arenal Volcano in Costa Rica produces numerous hot springs and is a place of geothermal activity. Meteoric water containing chloride, bicarbonate, sulfate, ammonia, and nitrogen from the atmosphere reacts with the minerals in the lava and tephra (ejected rocks and ash). The meteoric water with dissolved minerals seeps downward until it becomes heated from the volcano's interior and mixes with hot mineral water coming up from the volcano. Hot water reacts with volcanic materials, and this hot, mineral-rich water becomes buoyant while rising upward. It is then captured in the thermal hot spring pools.

Whether hot springs, salt caves, or energy vortices, the importance lies in spending time in these natural settings and charging our system. When our skin is electrically charged from the earth's healing modalities, we cleanse the energy fields that connect us with life force. One of the easiest ways to begin this process is barefoot in safe, transparent, grassy areas. Other forms of charging can occur while walking barefoot on a beach or hugging a tree. When we touch and feel natural objects in nature, we reduce stress and improve the immunity of our being.

SIGHT/SOUND/SMELL/TOUCH : SUNBATHING

As simple as it sounds, sunbathing is the process of getting outside. Whether that's lying down or sitting, the purpose is to be under the sun. According to the EPA, the average American spends 90 percent indoors. Nearly 80 percent of their life is inside buildings, and the other time is spent inside automobiles. This has led to a modern society deficient in vitamin D, making us more immune to colds and flu viruses and exposing us to higher concentrations of airborne pollutants.

Vitamin D is essential for our immune system; without it, our bones become thin and brittle. We need this vitamin to help our body absorb calcium and phosphorus, which are both crucial for the health of our bones. Without vitamin D, our physical stature weakens, impacting our mental state. A lack of vitamin D leads to anxiety, depression-like symptoms, a decline in cognitive health, and brain fog.

Sunlight also expands our blood vessels. As the blood vessels expand, our body releases nitrogen oxides stored within our organism. This not only lowers blood pressure but decreases the risk of heart disease. As a fluid movement of blood and oxygen flows through our body, we clear any blockage within the disks along our spine. From our root to our crown, when we experience flow, our state of being feels at ease. A feeling of freedom within the body illuminates the aura field into higher realms, moving us closer to higher consciousness.

If we don't spend enough time outside, we may experience hormonal imbalances. For example, serotonin is a hormone that elevates our mood and aids in maintaining a sense of calm.

Sunshine raises our bodies' serotonin levels, which is another reason some experience seasonal depression with the change from fall to winter months. When we experience fewer daylight hours, we tend to become moody and lethargic. This disconnect stunts the charging process our battery needs to expand consciousness. Modern humans must now consciously acquire exposure to the outdoors because we are new to this rising issue, an issue that occurred beneath our awareness during the urbanized focus in the Industrial Age.

Another occurrence began within the eighteenth to twentieth century, when we created daylight savings time. Pushing clocks forward to make greater use of daylight during the warmer months was used during World War I. It was an attempt for the globe to conserve energy. Researchers find it has only proven long-term adverse effects on our minds and bodies today. For instance, during the months we experience less time with the sun, we've seen heightened mood disturbances, hospital admissions, and raised inflammatory markers. Our desire to control nature misaligns our attachment to the world's natural rhythms, and we habitually become sick. We've continuously experienced this transaction by pretending to materially play God.

TASTE: WATER

There is nothing more essential to life on Earth than water. Our bodies are 60-80 percent water and play an essential role in carrying nutrients, removing waste, and digesting food. Water cools us when we're too hot and cushions our organs and joints for protection. When our characters are fully hydrated, we experience energy—an energy that clears our minds and heightens our awareness. In many cultures, water is used as a ritual to purify and cleanse the soul. Serving as a spiritual guide or protection, we seek out water in our lives for serenity.

Dr. Masaru Emoto was a Japanese researcher who became internationally recognized for his studies on the effects of consciousness and intention on water. He believed that water both stored and transmitted information, so much so that human emotion, thoughts, and words improved or degraded water quality.

Dr. Emoto exposed water to music, words, and images. He would then freeze the water and observe the crystal formations that emerged. When water was exposed to positive words and music, it would form magnificent, intricate crystals. When water was exposed to negative language and music, it became distorted and created chaotic crystals. He believed that water was not only a physical substance but had memory. Water could be influenced by human consciousness, and therefore, water could be used to promote healing within the world.

Water surrounds us in our oceans, lakes, rivers, and streams. We need water to survive, and it is crucial for many reasons: to regulate body temperature, prevent infections, maintain organ function, deliver nutrients to cells, and keep our joints lubricated. According to various studies, at least 50 percent of the world's population lives under water-stressed conditions for at least one month a year. In the modern world, we've created a global water crisis when we pollute our water or disconnect people from sanitized sources, which disrupts the evolution of humanity and all living organisms.

Water is a life force that reflects the human spirit and the interconnection of creation. We must treat our water with respect and kindness, as there is no more essential resource on the planet. On average, we should drink half our body weight in ounces daily to remain hydrated. Around the world, nearly two billion people live in environments where the water supply is inadequate. These alarming numbers stunt the evolution of human consciousness and our depth of awareness.

PART II: BUILD ENDURANCE

RESILIENCE

A glaring issue with modern life is our relationship with comfort. Technology that made life efficient also distanced us from the natural world. To reconnect, we need to put ourselves in stressful situations deliberately. The byproduct of exposure to deliberate stress gives our biological systems an ancestral connection. When we feel more human, we experience the adaptation required to move forward as a species. As modern life evolves, we must build a bigger capacity to handle stress. Navigating the material world, we will need endurance to expand consciousness. Use the following practices to build a resilient battery and experience the material world fully.

According to neuroscientist Andrew Huberman, when we force ourselves to embrace stress, such as cold or heat exposure, as a meaningful and self-directed challenge, we exert top-down control over deeper brain centers that regulate reflexive states. In this case, top-down refers to our idea of "resilience and grit." The prefrontal cortex is an area of focus in the brain that lights up, the area of the brain that directs our planning and suppresses impulsivity.

When we enter deliberate stress states, for example, a cold environment, we develop skills that carry over to situations in our lives. We cope and maintain a sense of calm to life's adversities. When confronted with real-world stressors, we experience a clear mind, which allows the prefrontal cortex to exercise rationale. In a world where we no longer hunt and gather or need fire to stay warm, it is critical to deliberately place ourselves into safe situations that trigger the most primal aspects of being a human.

When we build resilience and align deeper with the natural world, we direct our paths toward spiritual suffering. Our awareness grows, and we awaken the senses of our mind-body character. Using the following four practices to build tolerance to modern life strengthens the bond toward wholeness.

HIKING

Starting with a cardio activity, hiking is essential for our mind and body's health. Often, through hiking, we calibrate with our soul through the connection of nature. Therefore, hiking is best done in natural settings, whether near or around water or within a forest, open grassland, or mountain range. Our parasympathetic nervous system is engaged when our nervous system is stimulated by surrounding nature outside modern ailments such as populated areas, light pollution, air pollution, and noise pollution. With its engagement, our character adapts physically and mentally while the space provides freedom for the soul to experience reality.

Through movement, we experience higher heart rates, higher respiration rates, and general fatigue from exercise, but our nervous system begins to heal. This makes for a productive adaptation phase in our physiological processes. As these processes clear up and our entanglement with society unwinds, we start evolving into a healthier state of being.

As we move through nature, we are constantly challenged by unknown stimuli. We continually look for the next rock to step on, a branch to move, or a tree to climb. The unknown forces our mind to our primal instincts, making us feel more human. The moment creates a mindful practice and expands our energy field while hiking.

There is also a risk of danger; without a flat surface or paved roads, our nervous system is challenged to adapt. Exposure to fear involves our soul, which brings forth the state of becoming. As we navigate fear, our soul will attach to the character, and we will become closer to the source.

In a society that is obese, stressed, and mentally ill, we need cardio exercises to reduce such risks. Cardio training reduces the risk of heart disease, strokes, and high blood pressure and lowers cholesterol. As we hike up and down hills, our weight-bearing movements build muscle mass and prevent weak bone density. Our bodies thrive on the vitamin D the sunshine provides, which contributes to relaxation and enhanced well-being. These benefits drastically improve our endurance.

As studied, our mood and mental health improve in nature. The outdoors reduces stress, calms anxiety, and lowers our risk of depression. A study by the University of Stanford had participants walk for ninety minutes. One group walked in a grassland with oak trees and shrubs, while the other walked along a traffic-heavy four-lane roadway. The participants were then measured in categories such as heart rate, respiration rates, and brain scans.

The difference between the two groups showed up through neural activity in the subgenual prefrontal cortex. They found that the group that walked in nature showed a decrease in repetitive, negative thoughts and emotions versus those who walked in an urban environment. A clear difference within emotional regulation showed that being in nature lowered stress and improved mood compared to those in urban environments. We meet with our ancestral roots by moving and training our bodies to endure long distances in nature. Intentionally exposing ourselves to such practices curates an intuition only the soul understands. We acquire wisdom without words.

COLD EXPOSURE

There are many benefits to the practice of cold-water immersion (CWI) in human physiology. This practice dates to 3500 BCE, with Edwin Smith Papyrus making numerous references to cold being used for therapeutic purposes (Wang et al. 2006). Ancient Greeks were also known to practice CWI among their people. It was used as a therapy and for relaxation and socialization. Hippocrates made the statement, "The water can cure everything." He was using cold for medicinal purposes and analgesic benefits in the fourth century BCE (Tsoucalas et al. 2015).

Today, we know that deliberate cold exposure causes the release of epinephrine and norepinephrine, forms of adrenaline in the mind and body. These neurochemicals make us feel alert, and the cold can cause our levels to stay elevated for a significant amount of time following exposure. This allows us to work longer and more efficiently while maintaining a homeostatic and sustainable relationship with our health. Therefore, modern humans can benefit from CWI by increasing their energy and focus levels, which can be applied to mental and physical activities. As space opens and we lengthen material time, we substantially grow our vitality to have a spiritual journey within the human experience.

Cold exposure also releases dopamine, a potent molecule that elevates our moods. Dopamine is available for our character to enhance focus and attention, which directs our behaviors toward achieving goals. Regular use of CWI can sustain these elevations in our mood, energy, and focus, making this practice mainstream for the modern health of our species' rewilding process.

It is valuable to begin the process slowly to practice and improve an adaptation to cold. Start with short spurts of splashing cold water on the face and dipping both the hands and feet into buckets, sinks, or baths of cold water. Once these initial shocks become minimal, the intention should be to reach total body exposure where one can swim or sit comfortably in an uncomfortably cold-water environment.

The temperature of cold water can vary anywhere from fifty-nine to thirty-five degrees. Begin at a temperature you can handle while breathing through the nose only for forty-five to sixty seconds. Building up over time, one can expose themselves to lower temperatures and add time in which they are exposed to cold. Eventually, the timing and dosage of cold exposure become the pursuit of understanding oneself and deepening an individual's awareness.

HEAT EXPOSURE: SAUNA

It is believed the first saunas were built around 2,000 BCE, and the tradition of heat exposure originated in northern Europe. Countries today that broadly represent the practice include Estonia, Latvia, Russia, and Finland. It's hard not to think of Finland when considering saunas. With a population of just over five million, the small Scandinavian country is said to have an impressive three million saunas. In the compact country, there are more saunas than cars.

The first exposures to heat were made by man-made caves draped with animal skins and had a fire burning inside them during the day beneath a pile of stones. The fire would be put out, and smoke wafted outside. The rocks remained warm at night, and as people huddled inside, they poured water on the rocks to bask in the steam and sweat. Early saunas were sometimes the only place cold-weathered cultures could live. This is why an early-day sauna had multiple functions, such as kitchens and washrooms. A sauna could even serve as a hospital to heal the sick and give birth to babies. To the earliest sauna users, both the beginning and end of life occurred inside a sauna. For centuries, it had stabilized tradition, and heat became a valuable place for celebration.

Archaeologists even find evidence from saunas of the ancient world, like the Native American sweat lodges still used today. Ceremonies of the sweat lodge include rites of preparation, prayer, and purification. These sweat ceremonies involved heating stones until they were red hot, bringing them into the darkened chamber, and pouring water or aromatic herbal teas over them to punctuate the participants' rounds of fervent prayer. The heat and steam were meant to bring the tribe's people closer to the revelations of their souls and connect with the source. As we can imagine, the traditions became holy places that allowed us to worship.

Today, the sauna is a global experience. It is still used in social settings, but it has progressed into health clubs worldwide. From the general public to professional athletes, the health benefits of heat have brought longevity and clarity of mind to our human experience. Many studies have come forth, specifically from Finland, showing the value a sauna session has on our cardiovascular health. It lowers all-cause mortality and strengthens the resiliency of the modern-day nervous system.

The temperature of a sauna can vary from 165 to 200 degrees. The principles remain the same as those for cold exposure. It is essential to enter a temperature you can handle and maintain nasal breathing. Begin by starting at the lowest temperature and focusing on spending twelve to seventeen minutes in the sauna. Over time, each person can build up in both time and temperature. Compared to cold exposure, timing and dosage are everyone's individual pursuit of understanding.

NAIL BOARDS

A well-trusted practice with a long history resides in the principles of acupressure. For nearly 2,000 years, originating in India, devices used by yogis were called "Sadhu boards." These boards were a bed of nails used to stimulate energy points in the body. Today, you can find acupressure beds, straps, and mats online to mimic the ancient practice. There are also yoga boards that are made with high-quality wood, making them sturdy enough to stand on. The boards are typically assembled by hand with galvanized nails to avoid corroding.

According to early philosophies, our feet and palms had thousands of points linked to internal organs and the nervous system. The attention of such discoveries attracted other Eastern traditions, such as Chinese medicine. Working as a mirror to our inner landscape, when we stand, sit, or lay down on a bed of nails, we release endorphins, which increase blood and lymph circulation. This allows our body to self-regulate and eliminate pain while the mind receives a challenging dose of attention, enabling us to be mindful. As pain subsides and mindfulness enters our energy field, we create a space to explore the soul. It is a way to train the brain to remain calm under stress.

Despite our initial perception of discomfort, our connection through such modalities typically brings us closer to presence. The benefits are comparable to cold and heat exposure, as we force meditation by performing difficult, intentional tasks. We paradoxically experience relaxation and tranquility, a gateway to self-discovery. The experience can be a transformative journey that unlocks realms of consciousness.

When entering the nail boards, it is crucial to set an intention. Ask yourself what you're seeking. This helps with clarity and an experience that resonates with you. Second, it is vital to have a sense of reverence. One must approach the space with humility. Within the experience, focus on listening to your body and trust the wisdom flowing through you. Finally, you must appreciate a set of boundaries for yourself and incorporate a self-care environment. Follow the experience up with a silent meditation or journaling what you noticed. It may also be beneficial to slowly sit down briefly before taking a gentle and quiet walk. The purpose is to unwind slowly as you feel a deeper connection with the character and soul.

Begin slowly by standing on nails with socks on. This will alleviate the initial shock and allow the mind and body to build confidence. Focus on breathing through the nose calmly and staying on the nails for one minute. Perform three to five times weekly until you can comfortably stand on the nails for ten minutes. Once you have reached this point, start over, but this time, stand on the nails without socks. This may take a few weeks. The value is in taking your time and discovering your own awareness of the timing and dosage your mind and body need to align with the soul.

CHAPTER 10

THE CALL

A call for adventure.
Supernatural aid as we reach our threshold in the beginning.
Help is provided as the transformation begins.
Revelation (Death & Rebirth) takes place.
Final transformation and the return. With the return, we bring our gifts.
—The Hero's Journey, Joseph Campbell

We all have a calling, a feeling inside that guides us to pursue our potential. Often, frustration builds as we feel confused about what these feelings are. With the physical ease of life continuing to grow, we find ourselves stuck in our character, not knowing how to experience the soul. Without a feeling of wholeness, we cannot let the source in. The confusion seems relevant today, but maybe it's not. Perhaps we share contemplation with our ancestors because, without confusion, would there be any meaning to form our questions about existence?

For the duration of the book, the idea behind growth came in the form of questions. Contemplating life through the expression of our characters, we can connect and spiritually suffer, but where does progress lead? We must stop and ask, where is there? We all have a calling, but why do we feel compelled to share it with words?

An exercise used for centuries for personal and spiritual growth has been considered a labyrinth. A labyrinth is a complicated, irregular network of passages in which it is difficult to find one's way. Often mixed with a maze, the difference is in the meaning. A labyrinth is designed to foster contemplation and transformation, whereas a maze is typically put in place to confuse you.

Dating back thousands of years, labyrinth-formed circles were walked by those contemplating life—from religious and spiritual practices to the inside of hospitals, churches, and even the backyard or beach of today. A labyrinth has one entrance with one way in and one way out. The layout surrounding the center creates a maze, representing confusion and roadblocks along the journey. A symbolic form of pilgrimage, reaching the middle of the labyrinth stands for achievement, symbolizing the act of success and fulfillment.

To the generations before us, travel was not accessible. Many people could not afford to travel or explore the world, and they could not visit holy sites and lands. The labyrinths, coupled with prayer and contemplation, substituted for it. The significance eventually faded, and the maze-like figures began to serve as entertainment.

Recently, we've found a resurgence of the symbols' spiritual aspect in parks and wellness spaces that guide silent walks.

When someone is walking among the turnings, the intention is to lose track of direction and the material world, creating a state of mindfulness that quiets the state of being and welcomes the soul.

When our characters' minds are quiet and we're connected to our souls, we allow the source to come through. As the mind's eye activates and vibrates throughout the body, we feel a sense of adventure. Knowing that all potential needs action, the supernatural aids in the first movement. This is the beginning of our spiritual path. We begin to understand our life's work without words. Our energy field aligns with the higher consciousness as we realize the source created the cosmos, but the soul is the creator of the source. We can't explain these transformations, making our life's work an energy we intuitively express with God.

We uncover material skills we didn't think we had during a period of confusion. As momentum builds, the source shines within us, and the revelation occurs. We shed the material character and explore time with our actual awareness. We start to suffer spiritually and experience our calling. We are unable to convey this calling materially. Therefore, the soul plays a game with illusion as we audition the characters of the human experience with purpose.

ADVENTURE

When we spiritually suffer, we gain the potential of an evolved consciousness and collectively create a healthy material experience. Using our humanity's past as wisdom, the importance of living in harmony with our developed technology and the natural world seems imminent.

When we accelerated our ability to receive information and live with convenience, we found ourselves unhealthy and disconnected from the source. Without being equipped to handle the boom, the Industrial Age happened so quickly that it took until now to consider its determinants. A generation of people who can access all necessities by the touch of their finger is but a dream for our ancestors, and we are collectively lost.

Mentally and physically sick, we can't understand why. For centuries, our species plowed the way for a better life—a life that consisted of freedom from the threats of nature. Today, a population stands together as a single tribe, puzzled about learning each other's language. We're left with questions: What is the sustainable form of hierarchy? What is the meaning behind religion? Whose philosophy is the code to immaculate behavior?

Consumed by the terrors of our material world, we unconsciously believe we are above each other, convinced our way is right. Even worse, we never consider the opinion of the natural world. If we remain blinded by desire, we race to no finish line, consuming all available resources in hopes of silencing humanity's material suffering.

With a pause and a moment of stillness, maybe it's time we rewind. We must take steps to rewild our species, bring them back to the natural world, and suffer with the source. We should surrender our ambitions to the body of nature, the soul of God.

Our adventure would then become reconstructing and reorienting ourselves with the world around us, connecting with the natural world as our ancestors did and integrating the principles of nature into our polluted society. Awakening to the apocalypse of our planet, our adventure is to rewrite the cycle and spiritually suffer.

SUPERNATURAL AID

The power of source lives within us all, and we've reached the threshold. So, we call upon the aid of the supernatural to connect us to the soul and no longer live at the surface. It's time we ask big questions with tolerance for the traditions and cultures of our history. We must strip the characters we've played and immerse ourselves into the New World experience.

Ask, once more, who am I? We're met with a maze of frustration as we sit with no answer. Let's call upon God and ask for a feeling as we install within the pain of truth that showers over the soul. The surface of insecurity cannot be fixed with the fragileness of our material world. We are not the photos we share, the jobs we have, or the words we use. We are nothing beyond the characters who are here to experience. Therefore, we must spiritually suffer through the confusion of character and the voice of the material world.

We must remember that the soul wants wonder and craves awe. We are all artists at the core of source energy. Delivered upon good and evil, we are no different from the early rulers who needed assurance in their mission. Selling our pursuits materially, we're convinced the voice of God inspired our direction. Spiritually, the lesson is in learning that the gifts from the supernatural are to be shared with the cosmos, but our attachment cannot. We are not the result of our material work but pawns that influence the whole.

Therefore, we must let go and shine with the playing of our roles. Simultaneously, being aware of nothing because we are the beacon for the source, an alchemy to liberate change. As we place our unique imprint into the life cycle, our gift is to curate art from the soul into material. We must bring only what we have to the cause while sacrificing time with the character we play. Separating from materialism, we make our art for God.

DEATH, REBIRTH & THE RETURN

Death occurs at each checkpoint, shedding the character we once were—deeper into awareness, an experience only the soul has. Therefore, let yourself die in need of materialism and suffer with purpose. In search of truth, there is no war to fight besides our soul. Free from the chains of material identity, no hierarchy, religion, or philosophy narrates the depth of who we are.

We are here to cast the characters of humanity, playing them as children, existing with awe. We then experience the authentic presence of God, and the gifts our characters have are expressed through the soul. We may be puzzled by paradoxes; however, it is within order that we find the role that fits us. Play them with meaning as you add your touch of gold.

Without words, there can be no definition of who we are. Reborn to the consciousness, we find spiritual meaning in experience. Therefore, express the soul and break from the chains of structure as you see beyond the matrix of narration. Shed who you think you are and suffer with meaning while walking to God.

To ponder who I am? We're left without words . . .

Sincerely Yours, Harv

ACKNOWLEDGMENTS

I would like to acknowledge the love, support, and guidance from my family, friends, and colleagues. Special thanks to the individuals who directly impacted my work, such as Amy Scanlin. Without her guidance and editing, I would not have sustained a pursuit of quality work. I must acknowledge the depth of conversation I've shared with good friends such as Logan Gelbrich, Tommy La Stella, Nick Bjugstad, and Mitch Haniger. The commitment toward a better understanding has directly influenced my perspective and the inspiration within the pages of this book. Without the mentorship and guidance of Tim Brown, I would not have produced the content within these pages. For our friendship and commitment to the search, I thank you!

To my wife, Chelsea. The one who walks alongside me.

To my parents, Jim and Karen. My biggest fans.

To my sister, Jessica. My lifetime companion.

In all the moments I experience friction, I am reminded to persevere and continue because of you. For your love, courage, and strength, I move forward. Thank you!

BIBLIOGRAPHY OR REFERENCES

Kopnina, H., Washington, H., Taylor, B., & Piccolo, J. J. (2018). Anthropocentrism: More than Just a Misunderstood Problem. *Journal of Agricultural and Environmental Ethics, 31*(1), 109–127. https://doi.org/10.1007/s10806-018-9711-1

Studocu. (n.d.). *3. Worldviews for Geography - World views Human-centred Egocentric I am the most important creature - Studocu.* https://www.studocu.com/en-au/document/tara-anglican-school-for-girls/geography/3-worldviews-for-geography/22546379#

Richard Louv. (n.d.). *The Nature Principle - Overview - Richard Louv.* https://richardlouv.com/books/nature-principle/

Popedadmin. (2023, May 25). *What is Nature Deficit Disorder? Causes and Consequences - Population Education.* Population Education. https://populationeducation.org/what-is-nature-deficit-disorder-causes-and-consequences/

Warber, S. L., DeHudy, A. A., Bialko, M. F., Marselle, M. R., & Irvine, K. N. (2015). Addressing "Nature-Deficit Disorder": A mixed methods pilot study of young adults attending a wilderness camp. *Evidence-based Complementary and Alternative Medicine, 2015*, 1–13. https://doi.org/10.1155/2015/651827

Trewavas A. (2021). Awareness and integrated information theory identify plant meristems as sites of conscious activity. *Protoplasma, 258*(3), 673–679. https://doi.org/10.1007/s00709-021-01633-1

Ecosanctuary, Z. (2018, September 3). How nature benefits us through all our senses. *Zealandia*. https://www.visitzealandia.com/Whats-On/ArtMID/1150/ArticleID/144/How-Nature-Benefits160Us160Through160All-Our160Senses

World Health Organization: WHO. (2024b, August 7). *The top 10 causes of death*. https://www.who.int/news-room/fact-sheets/detail/the-top-10-causes-of-death

Environmental noise in Europe — 2020. (n.d.-b). European Environment Agency. https://www.eea.europa.eu/publications/environmental-noise-in-europe

Broccoli may help protect against respiratory conditions like asthma. (2009, March 9). ScienceDaily. https://www.sciencedaily.com/releases/2009/03/090302133218.htm

Beetroot juice helps lungs to work more efficiently. (2010, December 20). Nationalpost. https://nationalpost.com/news/beetroot-juice-helps-lungs-to-work-more-efficiently

Huberman, A. (2023, October 8). *The Science & Use of Cold Exposure for Health & Performance*. https://www.hubermanlab.

com/newsletter/the-science-and-use-of-cold-exposure-for-health-and-performance

Allan, R., Malone, J., Alexander, J., Vorajee, S., Ihsan, M., Gregson, W., Kwiecien, S., & Mawhinney, C. (2022). Cold for centuries: a brief history of cryotherapies to improve health, injury and post-exercise recovery. *European journal of applied physiology*, *122*(5), 1153–1162. https://doi.org/10.1007/s00421-022-04915-5

Oviir, A. (2019, August 6). Here's why the history of the sauna is deeper than you might think. *Medium*. https://medium.com/estoniansaunas/heres-why-the-history-of-the-sauna-is-deeper-than-you-might-think-d8e5127a8232

Stanford researchers find mental health prescription: Nature. (n.d.). Stanford University. https://news.stanford.edu/stories/2015/06/hiking-mental-health-063015

Sweat Lodge. (n.d.). The Pluralism Project. https://pluralism.org/sweat-lodge

Staff, T. (2015, June 25). Is world peace possible? *TIME*. https://time.com/3935254/is-world-peace-possible/https://time.com/3935254/is-world-peace-possible/

Abram, N. J., Mcgregor, H. V., Tierney, J. E., Evans, M. N., Mckay, N. P., Kaufman, D. S., Thirumalai, K. J., Martrat, B., Goosse, H., Phipps, S. J., Steig, E. J., Kilbourne, K. H., Saenger, C. P., Zinke, J., Addison, J. A., Leduc, G., Mortyn, P. G., Seidenkrantz, M. A., Sicre, M., . . . Von Gunten, L. (2016). Early onset of industrial-era warming across the oceans and continents. *Nature*, *536*(7617), 411–418. https://doi.org/10.1038/nature19082

Causes - NASA Science. (n.d.). https://science.nasa.gov/climate-change/causes/

Climate change the greatest threat the world has ever faced, UN expert warns. (2022). In *Ohchr*. United Nations Human Rights Office of the High Commissioner. Retrieved July 12, 2024, from https://www.ohchr.org/en/press-releases/2022/10/climate-change-greatest-threat-world-has-ever-faced-un-expert-warns

Glatter, K. A., & Finkelman, P. (2021). History of the Plague: An Ancient Pandemic for the Age of COVID-19. *The American journal of medicine, 134*(2), 176–181. https://doi.org/10.1016/j.amjmed.2020.08.019

History's seven deadliest plagues. (2024, May 27). https://www.gavi.org/vaccineswork/historys-seven-deadliest-plagues

What do primates have in common? humans & our cousins | AMNH. (n.d.). American Museum of Natural History. https://www.amnh.org/exhibitions/permanent/human-origins/understanding-our-past/living-primates

Penn, A. (2022, March 9). *Cognitive Revolution (Sapiens): How gossip changed our brains*. Shortform Books. https://www.shortform.com/blog/cognitive-revolution/

Scientific consensus - NASA Science. (n.d.). https://science.nasa.gov/climate-change/scientific-consensus/

Hassler, W. W., & Weber, J. L. (2024, August 3). *American Civil War | History, Summary, Dates, causes, map, timeline, battles, significance, & facts*. Encyclopedia Britannica. https://www.britannica.com/event/American-Civil-War

ushistory.org. (n.d.-b). *The American Revolution [ushistory. org]*. https://www.ushistory.org/us/11.asp#:~:text=In%20October%201781%2C%20the%20war,it%20official%3A%20America%20was%20independent

What is Globalization? Examples, Definition, Benefits and Effects. (2024b, March 25). Youmatter-dev. https://youmatter.world/en/definitions/definitions-globalization-definition-benefits-effects-examples/

Nash, J., PhD. (2024b, July 28). *The History of Meditation: Its Origins & Timeline*. PositivePsychology.com. https://positivepsychology.com/history-of-meditation/

www.ingramcontent.com/pod-product-compliance
Lightning Source LLC
LaVergne TN
LVHW091543070526
838199LV00002B/190